Jane Austen
& Adlestrop

HER OTHER FAMILY

Victoria Huxley is an editor and publisher who has lived in
Adlestrop for over twenty-five years. She is the co-author of
World Heritage Sites of Great Britain and Ireland.

D1465371

Jane Austen & Adlestrop

HER OTHER FAMILY

A new perspective on
Jane Austen and her novels

Victoria Huxley

Windrush Publishing
Gloucestershire

To Geoffrey, who first showed me the village and introduced me to country life

First published in Great Britain in 2013 by
WINDRUSH PUBLISHING SERVICES
Windrush House, 12 Main Street
Adlestrop, Moreton in Marsh
Gloucestershire GL56 0UN
01608 659328

Reprinted 2013, 2014 (twice)

ISBN 978-0-9575150-2-4
E-book available

Front cover: Portrait of Jane Austen by Cassandra Austen ©National Portrait Gallery, London and a 1831 engraving of Adlestrop Park.
Back cover: Watercolour sketch by Humphry Repton for the bath house in the flower garden at Adlestrop Park by permission of the Shakespeare Birthplace Trust

Cover by Mark-making Design
Maps by John Taylor
Typeset in Sabon 10.5 by Geoffrey Smith

Printed and bound in the UK by imprintdigital.com

www.janeaustenandadlestrop.wordpress.com

Table of Contents

Contents

Contents

Illustrations and Maps

INTRODUCTION

Jane Austen, Adlestrop and me

I first set foot in Adlestrop on a cold January day in 1985 to see a cottage that my partner (now husband) wanted to buy as a country weekend bolthole from, as he saw it, the horrors of London life.

He had just sold his own flat in London and had moved into my small terraced house in the city and therefore had some money to achieve his aim. Being a Londoner with little experience of country life I had no yearnings of my own to bring to his quest. However when he mentioned 'Adlestrop' I was immediately intrigued. Like many other people I remembered the Edward Thomas poem which for me imbued the village with a special aura of romance. A rural arcadia conjured up through beautiful verse.

On a late winter's afternoon twenty-five years ago I could see very little of the village, nothing of the cottage garden or its views but still found the unmodernised little house delightful. The ceilings were low, the wooden staircase very steep and there were lots of beams and tiny doorways and a huge stone fireplace. It had no central heating, needed rewiring, decorating and it only had a downstairs bathroom and loo, an awkward kitchen, small sitting room and two upstairs bedrooms. It had not been lived in for a year or more and was freezing cold.

As it was initially to be a weekend place and, at the time we just had one small toddler, I had no qualms about agreeing with him that it was ideal. A lease for one hundred and twenty years was duly signed with the Trustees of the Adlestrop Settlement in mid-June. By then the garden was knee-deep in nettles, forested with buttercups and dandelions and the dirt and cobwebs inside were formidable obstacles. However we came down when time allowed and got to work, called in a local firm of builders and decorators and moved in some old furniture. Two years later we decided to move completely into the village from London and it became our family home.

I cannot remember exactly when I discovered that Adlestrop had not just one literary connection but two. Perhaps it was the small booklet I found in Adlestrop church that alerted me to the fact that Jane Austen had come to the village at least three times to visit her cousin, the Reverend Thomas Leigh. Furthermore many scholars believe that one of the themes of *Mansfield Park* may have been based on her experiences at Adlestrop. I was thrilled to think that I could be actually walking where she must have trod – on the path to the church door for example – or on a country ramble to nearby Daylesford. But it was not until I had the leisure of semi-retirement and the departure of my three sons to university that I seriously began to research the Jane Austen connections with the village.

It was a trail that led me to the Gloucestershire archives, the Shakespeare Birthplace Trust in Stratford-on-Avon (where most of the Leigh family papers are kept), Stoneleigh Abbey, churches and burial grounds and asking questions everywhere. And it made me look anew not only at the village, but at Jane Austen and her life and gave me a fresh insight into my favourite reading matter – her novels.

I would like to thank my husband, Geoffrey Smith, first and foremost for all his encouragement and designing the layout of the book, and the help of (in no particular order) Lord Leigh, Ralph and Angela Price, Jinnie Holt, John Gillett, Janet Walker, John Taylor, Gillian Delaforce, David Hanks of Cotswold Images, Paula Cornwell and Cynthia Woodward at Stoneleigh Abbey, Alastair Williams at Mark-making Design, the staff of the Shakespeare Birthplace Trust, Gloucester Archives and Stow on the Wold Library, and David Selwyn at the Jane Austen Society. I would like to thank Francis Witts for his kind permission to quote from *The Complete Diary of a Cotswold Lady: The Lady of Rodborough, Agnes Witts, Volume One 1788-1793*. Any errors that exist are entirely of my own making.

Victoria Huxley
Adlestrop, December 2012

The Leigh and Austen Family Tree

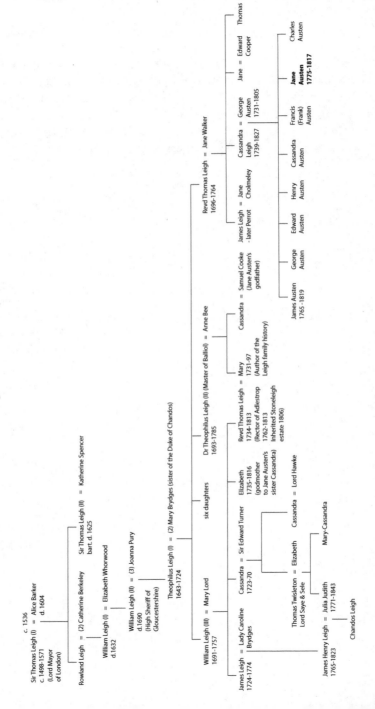

CHAPTER ONE

Adlestrop and the Austen Connection: The Leigh Family

'...descended from a long race of plain independent Country Gentlemen' **History of the Leigh Family: Mary Leigh**[1]

Young and impressionable, Jane Austen, first came to Adlestrop in 1794 when she was just nineteen, exchanging one vicarage in Hampshire to stay in another in this pretty corner of the Cotswolds. Why did she come to Adlestrop – a small and insignificant village in north Gloucestershire – and what were her family connections to this part of the world? The reasons are straightforward. Jane Austen's maternal grandfather, Thomas Leigh, was born there in 1696 and her mother was naturally keen to revisit her cousins and the happy memories of her childhood and for her own children to build bridges with the Leighs.

Adlestrop is the quintessential English village with its attractive country setting at the foot of a wooded hillside, the old houses fashioned in golden Cotswold stone, untroubled by modern traffic and looking as if nothing has changed for hundreds of years. It seems quite right that Jane Austen, the classic author of life in an English country village should be linked to Adlestrop.

Jane travelled with her mother and much-loved sister, Cassandra, and perhaps with one or more of her brothers. A year later she would begin to write 'Elinor and Marianne'(an early version of *Sense and Sensibility*) and the epistolary short

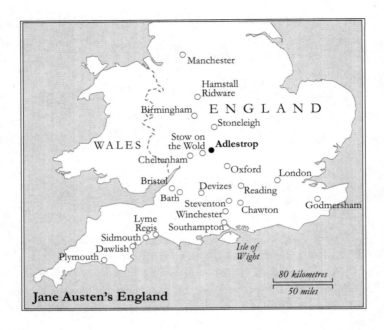

Jane Austen's England

novella *Lady Susan* but no one could have supposed at that moment that these writings were anything more than a suitable pastime for the daughter of a modest clergyman. There is also evidence in Jane's letters that Cassandra made further visits in 1813 and 1814.[2]

Jane was to become very well acquainted with Adlestrop and her cousins as she returned in 1799 and 1806 and, throughout her life, kept in constant touch with events there by letter. As the wise Lady Russell opines in *Persuasion* 'Family connections were always worth preserving'. And the cousins reciprocated and knew all the ins and outs of the Austen household. Mrs Austen relished the splendour of her Leigh heritage and their connections to lord mayors, duchesses and dukes and the titled branch of the family based at the great Stoneleigh Abbey estate in Warwickshire.

The Adlestrop Leighs were the senior branch of the Leigh

family and at Adlestrop they ruled the roost – big fish in a very small pond. One cousin was the rector, the other the owner of the mansion at Adlestrop Park and squire of the village and its environs. I believe that Jane's visits to Adlestrop and to the vast halls of Stoneleigh Abbey fired her imagination, and these places, her cousins and the history of the Leigh family became a rich source of material which she drew upon for some of her novels' plots and themes. In this book I will try to find out what the village was like in Jane Austen's time and I will delve into the background of the Leighs, look at the upheavals and changes that Jane saw take place in this backwater and how it all nourished her inquisitive mind.

'It was a sweet view — sweet to the eye and the mind. English verdure, English culture, English comfort...' Emma

———

First of all it is worth looking back into village history and how it was shaped by the Leigh family. Since Saxon times Adlestrop has been known by many different names: Aedelsthorp, Eadlesthorp, Tatlestrop, Tedestrop, Tadilthorpe, Attlesthorpe and Tiddlestrop until finally ending up with its present one. This literally means 'Tatel's thorp' – 'thorp' and 'throp' being interchangeable, derived from the Danish for a 'daughter settlement'. Who 'Tatel' was we will never know. Over the centuries the original 'T' was elided becoming Adlestrop which is now indelibly engraved on the nation's consciousness due to Edward Thomas's famous poem 'Adlestrop' which invokes an idyll that is the very essence of the English countryside. On a quiet summer's afternoon when there are few cars or people to disturb the peace, it is easy to take a romantic view of this lovely spot and imagine Jane and her sister sauntering down the lanes in their sprigged muslin frocks, pausing to admire the cottage gardens and the climbing roses and listening to birdsong. The view at the top end of the village where the church, Old Parsonage and Adlestrop Park stand in close proximity, overlooked by green horizons, is so unspoilt it feels as if it still belongs in an early arcadia.

The Leigh's influence on Adlestrop still holds in the twenty-first century: the current Lord Leigh lives in a nearby farm on the hill above the village and, through a trust, effectively still owns the freeholds of many of its houses plus substantial agricultural land holdings. The village is a symbol of the stability of English society and rural patterns. Many scholars believe that the eighteenth-century improvements carried out by Humphry Repton to the lay-out of the village, the landscaping of Adlestrop Park and the Old Parsonage and the Austens visit to Stoneleigh Abbey directly informed one of the themes of *Mansfield Park*.

'You are now collecting your people delightfully, getting them exactly into a spot as is the delight of my life; three or four families in a country village is the very thing to work on…' *Jane Austen in a letter to her favourite niece, Anna Lefroy née Austen, on the art of novel writing.*[3]

This is undoubtedly true but I have discovered many other significant echoes of Jane Austen's knowledge of Adlestrop and the Leighs, both in her letters and in her work. Jane Austen was such a consummate artist that she breathed life into her fictional characters, houses and villages without stooping to direct copying – but it is inevitable that events and people from her real world gave ballast to her imagined ones.

Jane Austen's novels were instantly popular when they were first written, admired for their literary merit and humour as well as their sharp perception of character and country ways. It is tempting to assume from a brief outline of Jane Austen's life and from the happy endings in her books that her own experience was without serious incident or excitement and that she was untouched by the greater issues of the time. In fact both her immediate and wider family offered her a rich spectacle of tragedies and extraordinary upheavals and she was also beset by the constant worry of financial insecurity, underlined by her status as a single woman of few means.

The Austen-Leigh family network was extensive with innumerable cousins, aunts and uncles, all in close touch with each other by letter and word of mouth. Without employment, many of the middle and upper classes passed their days by going on extended rounds of visits so that they could keep up with their relatives. Blood relationships were vital in a period when nepotism and connections counted for more than simple merit. A person's birth, their antecedents and their wealth all conferred respectability and a place in society. If you lost your reputation or your money or lacked the right stepping stones towards prosperity there was very little hope for you.

The Austen family were very conscious of their mother's ancestry and were brought up with family anecdotes about their eccentricities, noble marriages, and tragedies ringing in their ears. However, as so often, most of Jane Austen's biographers skate over the maternal line of descent although its history is far richer and more complex than that of the Austen line. One of Jane's cousins, Mary Leigh, wrote a history of the Leighs in 1788 just before Jane's first recorded visit to Adlestrop, and it is thanks to this rich source that many of the old stories about the family, their household and the villagers have survived. She dedicated the volume to the then 'Head of the Family' – the young James Henry Leigh stating:

> You wish me to collect all the anecdotes I can recollect and gather, of our Family… prepare yrself for much oral tradition; for old Womens legends, — for Ghosts & Goblins & for being extremely tired of the prolixity of my Dear Sir.[4]

A small flavour of her storytelling gifts can be seen from this introduction.

The history is written in a large volume bound in cream and gold with decorated endpapers that show a vignette of Adlestrop Park. Mary, then aged fifty-seven, wrote her narrative clearly and legibly on the left-hand side of each double page spread leaving the facing page for notes or for addenda often inserted by her husband or other family members. The volume found its way to Stoneleigh Abbey where it was used as a scrapbook by her descendants right up to the twentieth century, in which to paste letters, notes of family events and other memorabilia.

A Tudor portrait of a thin-lipped old man with a sharply pointed nose under a three-cornered black velvet hat hangs in the dark-panelled halls of Stoneleigh Abbey. His gown is trimmed with a wide fur collar and a golden chain. This is the face of Sir Thomas Leigh (c.1498–1571) the clever and hard-working founder of the family fortunes. Even then the Leighs were a well-placed dynasty: Thomas' brother William was an Usher to King Henry VIII and another brother had the same appointment in Queen Mary's court. But the younger son, Thomas, on leaving his Shropshire home sought a career in the world of the City of London where, after an apprenticeship, he became a freeman of the Mercers' Company.

The Mercers were a livery company that specialised in

'Then followed the history and rise of the ancient and respectable family…how it had been settled… how mentioned in Dugdale, serving the office of high sheriff, representing a borough in three successive parliaments, exertions of loyalty, and dignity of baronet, in the first year of Charles II with all the Marys and Elizabeths they had married…' *Persuasion* the importing and selling of luxury fabrics such as silks and velvets to the monarch and the aristocracy. They also engaged in the lucrative wool trade and dabbled on the foreign markets. Sir Thomas Gresham, Royal Agent and founder of the Royal Exchange was one of Thomas Leigh's contemporaries and also a Mercer. The Mercers were a byword for wealth and success at that time – perhaps their most famous member was the legendary Dick Whittington in the fourteenth century – another country boy from Gloucestershire who rose to become Lord Mayor of London.

Thomas made a very successful marriage in about 1536 to Alice Barker, the niece and heiress of an eminent fellow Mercer, Rowland Hill. Thomas Leigh continued to gain prominence in the company and also in civic life culminating with his election as Lord Mayor of London in 1558. He had the great honour of escorting the young Queen Elizabeth through the City of London during her coronation celebrations and was awarded a knighthood by her during his mayoralty. Further wealth was to follow when his wife's uncle appointed him a legatee and sole executor of his estates which included the roofless ruin of the old abbey at Stoneleigh. After the Dissolution King Henry VIII had donated this property to Charles Brandon, Duke of Suffolk and in 1561 Sir Rowland Hill purchased it.

The mid-sixteenth century was a good time to buy land when so many former religious estates were on the market after the Reformation and Thomas invested wisely. He already owned land in Gloucestershire at Longborough, a village some five miles from Adlestrop, courtesy of his marriage, and in 1553 he purchased the manor of Adlestrop from the Crown for the sum of £1,429.[5] In Elizabethan times a pound might correlate to £150 today so this was a substantial outlay if one does the multiplication: the equivalent of £215,000.

The previous owners of the village had been the abbots of Evesham Abbey which was settled by St Egwin, the third bishop of Worcester and consecrated by Pope Constantine in 709 –

a very early foundation. During its heyday it was one of the richest religious houses in England. In 718, a charter records the grant of six hides of land at Daeglesford (Daylesford) by Aethelwold, the king of Mercia, to the monastery. This land included Adlestrop as it covered the fields from the Bladen River (the Evenlode) right up to the Iron Age tumuli on the hill near to Chastleton where one of the mounds was excavated to reveal that it may have been a significant 'portal dolmen' dating back to 4000-3000 BC and, although badly ruined, still contained the ancient bones of at least three adults and four children.[6] Later charters record the village boundaries of Tatlestreow or Tatlestrop.[7]

By the time Sir Thomas died in 1571 he had amassed an enormous amount of land in Warwickshire, Gloucestershire and Leicestershire as well as valuable properties in London and Middlesex. It was his eldest son, Rowland, who inherited Adlestrop. Stoneleigh along with some other manors and the Hamstall Ridware estate in Staffordshire passed to his middle son, Thomas while the third son was given a Northamptonshire estate. However while the senior line at Adlestrop remained 'simple squires, the cadet line at Stoneleigh rose to a peerage'.[8]

What sort of influence did these country cousins have on Jane Austen? Both the Warwickshire and Gloucestershire Leighs were firm Royalists and supported the Stuart cause. This percolated down to Jane herself who as a young girl wrote of the Stuarts in her Goldsmith's *History of England* that they were, 'a family who were always ill-used, Betrayed and Neglected, whose virtues are seldom allowed, while their errors are never forgotten'. Her niece, Caroline Austen noted of her aunt:

> Of her historical opinions I am able to record thus much — that she was a most loyal adherent of Charles the Ist, and that she always encouraged my youthful belief in Mary Stuart's perfect innocence of all the crime with which History has charged her memory.[9]

Adlestrop Park was noted by Mary Leigh as 'a staunch asylum to every friend of the royalist cause'.[10] At Stoneleigh Abbey, the great grandson of Thomas and Alice, also named Sir Thomas Leigh, was a fervent defender of Charles I who sought refuge at Stoneleigh for three days in August 1642 after the gates of Coventry city were barred to him. In gratitude the king ennobled Thomas who became Baron Leigh in 1643. After the Civil War he may have regretted backing the losing side as he was forced to pay a huge fine of nearly £5,000 to Parliament. He only kept his liberty after assuring the victors that he had never borne arms nor helped the monarch with men or money.

Over the years the wealth of the Stoneleigh estate grew and in the 1750s the annual income from the estate of Thomas, the fourth Lord Leigh, was counted at £6,975.10s. 6d dwarfing that of Adlestrop which in the 1720s only had an income of £1,300. The strange turn of events that led to the poorer, but senior branch of the family inheriting the larger estates from the cadet branch were played out later in Jane Austen's own time when Stoneleigh's worth was put at around £17,000 a year – perhaps the annual equivalent of a million pounds in today's values. No wonder the impecunious widow of George Austen and her two unmarried daughters hoped that a few crumbs from this family magnificence might come their way.

It seems that some time after the Civil War ended William Leigh II,[11] a High Sheriff of Gloucestershire and leader of the local militia became the first Leigh to reside permanently at Adlestrop. It may have been the size of his family that forced this decision as he is reputed by Mary Leigh 'to have had 23 children' by three different wives; 'his son Theophilus used to say he had many elder brothers'. She speculates that William was 'perhaps drawn here by the beauties of the spot. This old house (pulled down for its want of stamina by yr father) was certainly fitted up at first in high stile; however forlorn in its latterday.'[12]

Perhaps the elder brothers did not survive Theophilus I

because he became the head of the Adlestrop branch and made an extremely advantageous second marriage to Mary Brydges, the sister of Lord Chandos. Lord Chandos had gained great wealth in his position of Paymaster General during the War of the Spanish Succession but he is chiefly remembered today as the patron of Handel who dedicated the beautiful Chandos Anthems to him. (A footnote to this distant connection to Jane Austen occurred in 1995 when Chandos House in London, a splendid Queen Anne mansion, was chosen as one of the locations for Ang Lee's film of *Sense and Sensibility*.)

The Chandos marriage also bought the name 'Cassandra' into the Leigh and Austen families from the maiden name of the second duchess: Cassandra Willoughby. The generous duke had a splendid mansion in Middlesex, known as 'Canons', and he would send for his nieces, the six sisters of Jane's grandfather, to be educated there and fix them up with marriage giving them 'dowries of £3,000 apiece'.[13] These sort of dowries could only be dreamt of by Jane and her sister, and also all her heroines.

Only a careful look at the family tree will help to sort out the different Leighs and their cousins as so many followed family tradition in their choice of Christian names: Cassandra, Jane, Elizabeth and Mary being popular ones for the women, and James, Thomas, Theophilus, William and Edward repeating themselves over the generations. (To aid the reader I have put I, II and III after the Williams and I and II after the two Theophiluses in the text.)

Theophilus Leigh I and Mary Brydges' marriage was a happy one:

> they resided almost intirely at Adlestrop, living in a very hospitable and liberal stile: nor was Charity neglected; the poor in this and neighbouring villages, with eight persons from Stow, every day after dinner, shared the remnants of the plentiful Table.[14]

In her history Mary Leigh sets the scene as it was during this first Theophilus Leigh's tenure of Adlestrop Park who was, by all accounts, extremely formidable and old-fashioned – perhaps reminiscent of General Tilney of *Northanger Abbey* in his rigid dining habits: 'The dinner was the same every day in each week (allowing for Seasons) & his Sons took care to ride from Oxford to meet the Thursdays boiled Rump....' The beef must have been special because although Adlestrop is only about twenty miles distant from the city it would still have taken a good couple of hours in the saddle.

Theophilus I had six sons and six daughters, but just three of the sons concern us: the eldest, William III and two younger brothers: Theophilus II and Thomas – Jane Austen's grandfather. William III would inherit the Adlestrop estate while Theophilus II and Thomas were both Oxford graduates destined for the church. Theophilus II was a high-flyer who was voted in as Master of Balliol, largely because he was the nephew of a duke, but thanks to his longevity and wit, became a notable member of the University. He also held the living at Adlestrop church but due to his position in Oxford left his parish duties in the care of a curate. This seems to have caused some friction between him and his father:

His Son, Dr Leigh had been Rector of this Place (of which Mr Parsons was Curate) many years before he ventured to ascend the pulpit: he did it unasked. Mr Leigh immediately got up, and turned his back upon the Divine; who expected a sharp reprimand awaited him; but on coming out of Church, his Father only said, "I thank you Theo, for yr discourse; let us hereafter have less Rhetoric and more Divinity: I turned my back lest my Presence might daunt you." [15]

Theophilus I was a serious man given to much thought on religion and other matters of the day:

His mornings were spent in his Study (for he read much)
& the evening never was perhaps so satisfactorily spent as
when he could engage his Chaplain in a free and liberal
dispute.[16]

At Adlestrop Park the chaplain or curate was held in high
regard unlike the snobbish Sir Walter Elliott's opinions in
Persuasion:

Wentworth? Oh ay! Mr Wentworth, the curate of
Monkford. You misled me by the term *gentleman*. I
thought you were speaking of some man of property: Mr
Wentworth was a nobody, I remember; quite unconnected.

Not much is known about Jane Austen's grandfather, Thomas,
the youngest son, except that like his brothers he enjoyed the
fruits of an Oxford education and no doubt rode over with
them to partake in the famous 'boiled rump' at his father's
table on a Thursday. He missed out on the estate and the family church living, but had his moment of glory when he was
elected a fellow of All Souls College at such a young age that
he carried the affectionate nickname of 'Chick' Leigh ever
after. He then took Holy Orders and became the rector of
Harpsden, near Henley-on-Thames, moving away from
Gloucestershire. Mary Leigh describes

'I do not know when I have heard a discourse more to my mind...or one better delivered – He reads extremely well, with great propriety and in a very impressive manner...I own I do not like much action in the pulpit — I do not like the studied air and artificial inflexions of voice, which your very popular and most admired preachers generally have. — A simple delivery is much better calculated to inspire devotion, and shows a much better taste.' *The Watsons* her uncle as 'one of the most contented, quiet, sweet-tempered, generous, cheerful men I ever knew'. His character was in great contrast to his flamboyant brother and bombastic father.

The wife Thomas chose, Jane Walker, was a member of the wealthy Perrot family, and it was the unequal division of the inheritance of the Perrot fortune between their children: James, Cassandra (Jane Austen's mother) and Jane (Jane Austen's aunt) that was to cause so much friction during Jane Austen's lifetime. In a turn of events, worthy of any novel, Jane Walker's aunt, Ann Perrot:

> ...earnestly begged her brother, Mr Thomas Perrot, to alter his will by which he had bequeathed to her his estates... and to leave her instead an annuity of one hundred pounds. Her brother complied with her request, and by a codicil devised the estates to his great-nephew James, son of the Rev. Thomas Leigh, on condition that he took the surname and arms of Perrot.[17]

(In an almost exact parallel, Jane Austen's brother Edward was adopted by a wealthy childless couple, the Knights, changing his surname from Austen to Knight and living in comparative luxury to his siblings.)

Cassandra Leigh and her sister, Jane, merely inherited two hundred pounds each and, although they were noted beauties, both married impecunious clergymen – George Austen and Dr Edward Cooper respectively. Cassandra did not think herself a beauty although she boasted a distinguished aristocratic profile and was noted for her sharp sense of the ridiculous, mental acuity and a facility for writing verse. A formidable woman in all respects.

Cassandra had another brother too – this fourth child was born in 1747 and named after his father, Thomas. The child was described as an 'imbecile' and, as customary for the age, was not cared for within the family home. History repeated itself when Cassandra and George Austen had their own backward and epileptic son, George, who later joined his uncle to be looked after by a local family at Monk Sherborne in Hampshire. Jane mentions neither this uncle nor her brother in any of her correspondence. Her brother George lived to be seventy-two.

It was a family tradition amongst the Austens that Cassandra Leigh may have met her husband while staying with her uncle, Theophilus II at the Master's Lodge in Oxford, although we have no direct proof or information about their courtship. George Austen was a Fellow at St John's College. Cassandra would also have come into close contact with Theophilus' daughter, Mary, the author of the family history. Biographers believe that Jane's mother was more likely to have inherited her wit and incisive turn of phrase from Theophilus II than from her own father. Theophilus II was certainly a valuable family connection in the Austens' fortunes and was celebrated among his contemporaries at Oxford as a great wag and raconteur. A famous *bon-mot,* repeated at the Austen dinner table, related how, on hearing that a colleague had been 'egged on' to marriage, Theophilus commented: 'Let us hope the yoke will sit lightly upon him.'

When James Austen (Jane's eldest brother) was enrolled at St John's College he and his father had dinner, presumably at the Master's Lodge, with the old man – then eighty-six. Still as sharp as a pin, Theophilus remarked when James took off his gown before eating: 'Young man, you need not strip, we are not going to fight.'

As already noted Theophilus II was an absentee incumbent and only lived in Adlestrop during the long college vacations. He rarely took the service in the church – all its offices would have been undertaken by the curate, the aptly named Mr Parsons, who was also the domestic chaplain to the family and servants of Adlestrop Park. His elder brother William III inherited the estate but it was not to be an easy succession as their father's death in 1724 exposed crippling debts accruing to the property. It seemed that the estate could be lost entirely. Mary Leigh gives a dramatic report of the causes and the events that then unfolded:

> the unavoidable effect of a large family, and all from an estate not then [worth] more than £1300 per ann. — nothing could be more deranged than the family affairs. Longbro. Estate only was settled — therefore poor dear, devoted old Adlestrop was doomed to be sold!
> "No" (said yr exemplary Grandmother Leigh) "Let not that favored Place be alienated from the family, let us give up all our income, receiving a stipend sufficient to support us properly abroad, place the estates at nurse, & reside in Holland (a country in which Mr Leigh is much known) then we can return with ease & a gay conscience into England"... Under the fostering care of the worthy old Chaplain Mr Parsons, the estate was placed, the house being let & everything put on the most economic plan from the year 27 to 32. Mr Leigh resided at Utrecht and his good wife used to say no part of her life was more satisfactory or pleasant. [18]

William III and his wife returned to Adlestrop from Holland with their finances on a more even footing, bringing with them their eldest son James aged about seven. Disaster had been averted. It is of course in *Persuasion* that Sir Walter Elliot is forced to let his ancestral pile, Kellynch Hall, and move to Bath to retrench and cover his debts and is cuttingly described as 'a foolish, spendthrift baronet, who had not had principle or sense enough to maintain himself in the situation in which Providence had placed him'.[19] The young Cassandra Leigh must have often heard of her cousins' forced sojourn on the Continent and the happy ending of their successful return to Adlestrop.

No retrenchment was necessary at Stoneleigh Abbey where

the family had recovered from their debts in the seventeenth century and were prosperous enough for the fourth Lord Leigh, after marrying an heiress, to build a new and magnificent West Wing to the house. It is striking that the Adlestrop Leighs did not seek any help from this quarter although they kept in contact. Jane Austen's grandfather would ride over to Stoneleigh on a summer's day accompanying his elder brother to visit their noble cousins and exchange news. All was set fair at Stoneleigh Abbey until an unexpected tragedy was to strike the whole family in the late eighteenth century, the unravelling of which would uncannily coincide with Jane Austen's last visit to Gloucestershire.

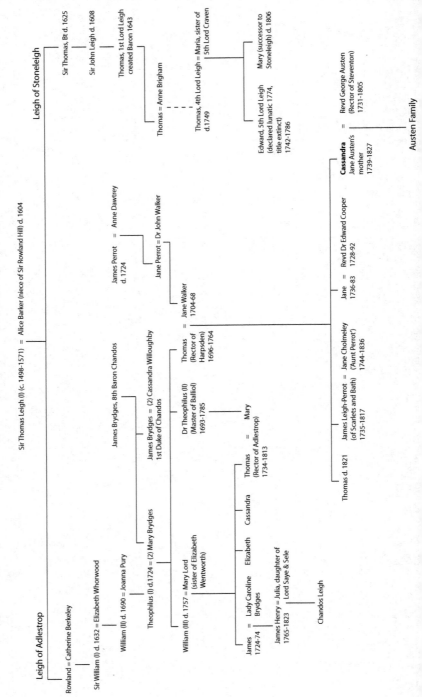

The Leighs of Stoneleigh and Adlestrop

CHAPTER TWO

Country Cousins: Aristocrats and Squires

'Cassandra (the second daughter of Thomas Leigh & Wife of the truly respectable Mr Austen) has eight children: James, George, Edward, Henry, Francis, Charles, Cassandra & Jane.' **History of the Leigh Family: Mary Leigh**[1]

W ho were the Leighs at Adlestrop and Stoneleigh whom Jane Austen met and was familiar with? These were the descendants of William III and Mary née Lord – four of whose children play a part in this story: Cassandra, James, Thomas and Elizabeth. Jane was directly affected by their sagas of dynastic marriages, untimely deaths and mental instability, their quest for fashionable improvements, their money struggles and quarrels over inheritance.

At their home in Steventon, the Austen family were well-respected members of their community due to their father's position as vicar, but in Adlestrop Jane Austen observed her cousins enjoying total sway in the great house, as well as in the pulpit, all bolstered by the financial benefits of their landownership. The parsonage inhabited by her childless uncle and his wife and sister must have seemed quiet and a little dull after her own home crowded with her brothers and her father's pupils. But Adlestrop had the advantage of a wonderful setting, accessible walks and rambles. There were three Leighs at the parsonage who Jane would come to know well.

The Reverend Thomas Leigh

Jane did not have a chance to meet her grand cousin, James Leigh, as he died at the relatively early age of forty-nine in 1774, but from that generation she had a close relationship with James' brother, the Revd Thomas Leigh who held the family living of Adlestrop church for an amazing fifty-one years residing with his wife, Mary, and later with his unmarried younger sister, Elizabeth. Close and continual links with the Austens and their children were maintained between the two families. The Revd Thomas was godfather to Jane's favourite elder brother, Henry, and Elizabeth was godmother to her only sister, Cassandra. Jane characterised the Revd Thomas as 'worthy, clever, and agreeable'.

'Of Thomas the 3rd son of William Leigh, it becomes this flippant and well inked pen to be laconic – for of all men living he most dislikes praise…. after Evesham School to Balliol and from thence to Magdalen College (where he resided with fair fame) till the year 62. He then became Parson of Adlestrop.' *Mary Leigh's Family History* [2]

Jane had come across him since she was a small child, as Thomas, when a young man, had often stayed with the family at Steventon and was much liked for giving the boys a small present of money. Another glimpse of his involvement with Jane was his visit to her and Cassandra during their schooldays at the Abbey School in Reading – Jane would have been about eight at the time. Their kindly cousin entrusted them with half a guinea each.

Whenever Jane and her family visited Adlestrop they always stayed at the handsome and well-appointed parsonage rather than at Adlestrop Park. It is unfortunate that Jane left no record in the form of letters of her impressions or activities at Adlestrop because she always visited the village in the company of her sister and mother who were her main recipients. Another issue is that only twenty-eight of her letters survived Cassandra's bonfire from the period between 1796 and 1801.

The Leigh's parsonage was considerably grander than Steventon's with more servants and household help than the Austens enjoyed. In 1805 when the Revd Leigh was preparing his 'Statement of Property' for the Commissioners – an early form of a tax return – he appends to the accounting of the money he has, including £513 a year earned in interest from his investments, a list of 'persons resident in my house'[3]. His sister, Elizabeth Leigh and his niece the Dowager Lady Saye & Sele are noted and against her name he is careful to inform the Commissioners that she will be making her own statement via her own attorney later. He also lists the 'Servants in my house' which include the butler, Mr Rainbow, two livery servants, a gardener and his helper (who are not resident) and five women servants, including Rebekah Cadwallader whom Jane mentions in a letter in 1809.[4]

The Revd Thomas Leigh was a huge influence on the village and always in residence, recording in his meticulous hand every birth, wedding and death that took place among his parishioners. In this he resembled Jane's father who had a similar hands-on approach and was also well-read and cultured. Thomas also took on the role of guardian to his nephew, the young James Henry Leigh who was left without his father at the tender age of nine. The other guardian was the third Duke of Chandos, James Henry's maternal uncle. After his father's untimely demise James Henry and his mother, Lady Caroline Brydges, lived largely with her relations and Adlestrop Park was let, which meant that Thomas had to take responsibility for all the Leigh affairs during this period. The stability that the Leighs gave the village and the strong roots they had there would have met with Jane's wholehearted approval. Her fictional villages and characters are strongly drawn, but it is not the places that matter in themselves but the values of the people who live there. A fine estate like Norland in *Sense and Sensibility* and its importance in the surrounding community are jeopardised with a change in ownership – even though the hereditary rule applied – from a benevolent and well respected landlord to one who, together with his wife, was 'narrow-minded and selfish'. Here at Adlestrop was a family who knew their position carried with it responsibilities and duties as exemplified by the long years of Thomas Leigh's service.

The 1770s were a difficult time for both branches of the Leigh family. Disturbing news came from Stoneleigh concerning Edward, the fifth Lord Leigh. In his twenties he seemed to have been the perfect model of an aristocratic young man. After matriculating at Oriel College, Oxford in 1761 and receiving an MA in 1764, he lived at Stoneleigh Abbey where he was able to indulge his interests in literature, music and science. However he also went out into the wider world and took up his seat in the House of Lords and attended the coronation of George III.[5] Edward's trustees were assured in a letter from the Lord Chancellor that his Oxford studies were carried out with diligence and at twenty-five he was elected High Steward of the University of Oxford and also a Doctor of Civil Law.

In his will he left his library of outstanding works on architecture and music, his scientific instruments, maps and prints to Oriel. Numbering about a thousand volumes, described as being of 'unusual magnificence' by the college, a new library (now known as the Senior Library) was built at Oriel to house the collection. A study of family papers 'show the books in a fascinating light...of the wider interests of a gentleman virtuoso and connoisseur'[6] but, of course, the library at Stoneleigh was left sadly empty – a fact much lamented by his successors who saw the remaining volumes in Virgil's memorable phrase: '*rari nantes in gurgito vasto*' – 'a few figures lost in the waves'.

Edward shared the Abbey with his elder sister, the Honourable Mary Leigh, and was a superb custodian of the house undertaking imaginative modernisation and refurbishment of the interior, as well as managing all the business of the estate once he came of age. His greatest achievement was the planning of the splendid hall, now called the Saloon, decorated with beautiful plasterwork illustrating the exploits of Hercules. Edward was deeply interested in architecture and made many drawings on the subject in his own hand including ideas for altering Francis Smith's stolid façade at Stoneleigh – one of which was a scheme to 'Gothicize' it, aping the frontage of Adlestrop Park by Sanderson Miller.[7] This is interesting as it looks as if Edward studied it and appreciated it *in situ*.

Edward was keen on horse racing, hunting and other country pursuits. When he decided to round off his education by embarking on a Grand Tour of the Continent in 1767 it may be that he only made a short visit to France worried by encroaching ill health. It was then he prudently made his will in case of misadventure. All was not entirely as it seemed, as Edward consulted one of the eminent doctors of his time, Dr John Monro, who specialised in mental health. Records show that Monro was paid £49.7s. for visiting Lord Leigh seventeen times in London and six times in Warwickshire.

There are no descriptions of exactly how Edward's mind was affected, but over the next few years he saw Dr Monro regularly and then Francis Willis who was engaged to care for him. Both Monro and Willis were prominent in their field and later involved with the treatment of King George III's fragile mental state. Willis had a private asylum in Lincolnshire where Lord Leigh spent some three years of his life in the early 1770s and was charged £105 a month in fees. Willis with his 'piercing gaze' kept no notes on any of his patients and his methods of treatment are hazy, although he claimed success for nine out of ten of his patients.

Edward Leigh's fine mind deteriorated to such an extent that his distressed family and friends applied to the Lunacy Commission for the right to manage his estates and he was declared a lunatic in March 1774 through an Inquisition into Insanity. The local papers noted: 'his Lordship was of unsound mind, and had not for several years been capable of managing his very noble estate and fortune.'[8] His sister Mary was left as life tenant of Stoneleigh and his will stated that if she or her half-sister failed to produce an heir the estate would pass 'to the first and nearest of my kindred being male and of my name and blood that shall be living at the time of my determination of the several estates'.[9]

This rather vague and unsatisfactory wording in the will put every male Leigh connection to thinking that they might inherit at some future date although the Hon. Mary Leigh, then thirty-eight, or her half-sister might still marry and who could know how long she might live? Or Edward might recover and sire an heir. There is no doubt that the Leighs of Adlestrop, especially the Revd Thomas Leigh, in his role as guardian to his nephew, must have considered themselves very much the favourites in a claim to any inheritance. In the Austen household the nearest male kindred was Mrs Austen's brother – James Leigh Perrot – just a year younger than his cousin in Adlestrop, and both were comparatively elderly and childless, conditions that would naturally incite a certain feverish amount of hopeful conjecture. In 1787 Leigh Perrot wasted no time in voicing his demands, seemingly believing that he had the greatest claim on the estate. He first proposed that the Stoneleigh estate bequest should be split into eighteen parts with twelve-eighteenths to go to him and his heirs and the remaining six-eighteenths to Thomas Leigh.[10] The Hon. Mary Leigh would not countenance breaking up the estate but still Leigh Perrot made what his cousins considered unreasonable demands such as being paid £50,000 in ready money to give up his claim or 'in order to accommodate the family' was willing to accept an annuity instead.[11] Thomas Leigh thought that Leigh Perrot was deeply ungrateful to the Hon. Mary Leigh and wrote to James Henry on 20 February 1787 that Leigh Perrot was 'not at all solicitous to pay that respect of gratitude, wh[ic]h her attention to our family & to himself in particular, in proposing to distribute her rights amongst us, deserved.'[12] His postscript summed up exactly what he thought of Leigh Perrot although shrewdly he advised discretion and forbearance on the issue:

'Tho we can but think very unfavourably of Mr Perrot's behaviour, we had better keep our sentiments to ourselves, lest an open rupture ensue; which can answer no good end; will only exasperate; & obstruct any possible future negociation; or embitter a lawsuit, shd such arise.'[13]

It was left until the Hon. Mary Leigh's death in 1806 for a resolution between Jane's relatives but in the meanwhile the dispute simmered dangerously in the background for all concerned.

———

For the last thirteen years of his unhappy existence, Edward was brought back to Stoneleigh Abbey to live under restraint and, cared for by a full-time resident surgeon-apothecary, James Butler, who was the brother of the estate's agent.[14] Here right at the heart of the Leigh family was a plot from a sensational Gothic novel – but an event that Jane Austen never alluded to. Madness or mental incapacity such as that found even nearer home with her own brother and uncle characterised as 'imbeciles' was too dark a subject to be aired.

The news of Edward's tragic condition was greeted with sadness at Adlestrop as both Theophilus II and his brother, Revd Thomas, had known the young aristocrat well, had visited him

'Catherine as she crossed the hall, listened to the tempest with sensations of awe; and when she heard it rage round a corner of the ancient building, and close with sudden fury a distant door, felt for the first time that she was really in an Abbey...they brought to her recollection a countless variety of dreadful situations and horrid scenes.' *Northanger Abbey*

at Stoneleigh, certainly as early as 1767, and kept in regular touch with him.[15] Elsewhere the loose framing of the will led to many attempts of other more distant Leighs to claim their being 'kindred' and would cause litigation well into the nineteenth century. Jane herself was born in 1775 and her lordly cousin's condition and the conditions of the will were part of family lore – a perpetual murmur during her upbringing.

Is it any wonder that the issue of inheritance and the fairness of wills and the sharing of family wealth are major themes in both *Sense and Sensibility* and *Pride and Prejudice*?

There was no time for distractions at Adlestrop Rectory where Revd Leigh, in contrast to his eminent father-in-law, was a man that Sir Thomas Bertram might have approved of. In *Mansfield Park* Sir Thomas lectures the cynical Henry Crawford on the lifestyle of the ideal clergyman:

> ...a parish has wants and claims which can be known only
> as a clergyman constantly resident, and which no proxy
> can be capable of satisfying to the same extent. Edmund
> might, in the common phrase, do the duty of Thornton,
> that is, he might read prayers and preach, without giving
> up Mansfield Park; he might ride over, every Sunday to a
> house nominally inhabited, and go through divine service;
> he might be the clergyman of Thornton Lacey every
> seventh day, for three or four hours, if that would content

him. But it will not. He knows that human nature needs more lessons than a weekly sermon can convey, and that if he does not live among his parishioners and prove himself by constant attention their well-wisher and friend, he does very little either for their good or his own.[16]

It was the Reverend who led the way in the changes and improvements to the grounds of his rectory (see pages 66-68), helped his brother, James, to do the same and later encouraged his nephew to undertake further upheavals. This was not an unusual preoccupation for a clergyman – at least sixteen of his contemporaries put pen to paper on the subject of the ideal garden, which most likened to the Garden of Eden veering away from the formalised structures of the previous century.[17]

Like Edmund Bertram and Jane's own father here was the younger son of an eminent family becoming a clergyman with the gift of a family living – not with reluctance but embracing it as a calling. He was perhaps in a minority. An amusing spoof in James Austen's university magazine, *The Loiterer*, mocked how many of his undergraduate acquaintances had become ordained and how bleak their lives would be afterwards:

> 'The rector of a parish has much to do.— In the first place, he must make such an agreement for tythes as may be beneficial to himself and not offensive to his patron. He must write his own sermons; and the time that remains will not be too much for parish duties, and the care and improvement of his dwelling, which he cannot be excused making as comfortable as possible.'
> *Pride and Prejudice*
> *Mr Collins on his duties*

Young men in the bloom of life, and the Heyday of their blood, cut off from all that renders life agreeable, removed for the Scene of their triumphs... condemned to pass many years in solitary obscurity and insipid quiet... for in spite of all the fine things which Poets, both ancient and modern, have said on the charms of Solitude, and the happiness of Country Life, an impartial examination of the matter will convince us, that a dirty Village is not half so good a place to lounge in as the High Street.[18]

Thomas was lucky in that the 'dirty Village' he ministered to was his home and he undoubtedly had a strong sense of duty to his parishioners. Many of Jane Austen's fictional clergy seemed to have an incredible amount of leisure time and indeed they were a lot less busy than their modern counterparts. Even on a Sunday the number of church services they were expected to officiate at had diminished over the eighteenth century. In the 1700s prayers were required to be read twice on Sunday probably around ten in the morning and mid-afternoon with a long sermon during at least one of these services. In between times the clergyman would be involved in the churching of women after childbirth, hearing the children go over their catechism and preparing them for Confirmation. However as pluralism grew, the giving of two sermons became difficult and one of the services was discontinued. Holy Communion was unlikely to be practised more than once a month in a country parish. In Adlestrop the population was growing in the period of the Revd Leigh's tenure and there were many baptisms, weddings and funerals to be attended to.

Thomas was certainly as a man of great energy, perhaps impatient at being confined to a small parish, a scholar yet one also concerned with practicalities. The secular matters of tithes, rents and roads all took up his time as well as his clerical tasks. It is doubtful that he ever had an idle hour and in his seventies, when he might have enjoyed a peaceful retirement, he had to wrestle with the vexed issue of the Stoneleigh inheritance (see pp. 113-126).

When he died Jane wrote about him with great affection in a letter to her brother Frank on HMS *Elephant* on 8 July 1813:

> ...the respectable, worthy, clever, agreeable Mr Tho. Leigh
> who has just closed a good life at the age of 79 & must have
> died the possessor of one of the finest Estates in England
> & of more worthless Nephews and Neices (sic) than any
> other private man in the united Kingdoms.[19]

Perhaps the barb at the end of the sentence about the more
'worthless Nephews and Neices' heightens the fact that
nothing of his inheritance came down to them, although
he was a cousin rather than an uncle. Or, if meant literally,
it could refer to James Henry Leigh and his wife, but that is
probably not what Jane Austen intended.

There is a memorial tablet to him in Adlestrop church
honouring his long contribution as rector and he is buried with
his wife, Mary Leigh.

> Reverend Thomas Leigh, formerly of Magdalen College,
> Oxford and 51 years rector of this parish. B. July 1 1734 d.
> June 26 1813. Also in same vault, Mary Leigh daughter of
> Rev Dr Leigh, master of Baliol College and the Affectionate
> wife of said Rev. Thomas Leigh, youngest son of William
> Leigh Esquire b. 20 July 1731 d. 9 February 1797 and in
> family vault adjoining Elizabeth Leigh d. of William Leigh
> b. November 17 1733 d. 18 April 1816

Mary Leigh
'She wrote some novels highly moral & entertaining.' **Note
by her husband[20]**

Jane's first hostess at Adlestrop Rectory was Mary Leigh, a
first cousin and old friend of her mother's. It was not until she
was in her early thirties in 1762 that Mary Leigh, the daughter
of the Master of Balliol, was to marry her cousin, Thomas,
who was three years her junior. We do not know if it was a
love match or simply a convenient one for both sides of the

family but judging from her husband's comments after her death (see below) it seems to have been a happy one. They had no children and because of this took a very close interest in all their other relatives – especially the young heir to Adlestrop Park, James Henry Leigh.

To both Mary and Thomas, Adlestrop would have already been familiar and felt like home but one wonders how Mary, after the bustle of Oxford and college life felt about removing to such a small and quiet place. On their marriage, her father, Theophilus II, gave up the church living which James Leigh duly passed to his brother and the newly-weds moved into the parsonage. Dr Leigh meanwhile took up another living in Somerset but according to his daughter 'spent much of his time with them in a darling abode amid a social neighbourhood'.[21] Just before he died in 1785 Mary wrote from Balliol to her nephew's wife, Julia who was then staying at Bath, about her father,

> Dr Leigh is free from all bodily complaints. That in his 92nd year his intellects are perfectly clear, but that he is weak and infirm, and at times his fine spirits a little flag.[22]

Mary's family history is an interesting compilation that must have taken her at least a year or more to research and complete. It demonstrates her clear and intelligent mind and also a garrulous propensity for amusing old stories; her love of Adlestrop and the Leigh family shines through. I daresay she may have bored all her guests with readings from it – or certainly presented them with the volume to look through. I wonder what Jane thought of Mary's description of her own family:

> Cassandra (the second daughter of Thomas Leigh & Wife of the truly respectable Mr Austen) has eight children: James, George, Edward, Henry, Francis, Charles, Cassandra & Jane. With his sons (promising to make figures in

life) Mr Austen educates a few youths of chosen friends and acquaintances. When amongst this liberal society, the simplicity of hospitality & taste which commonly prevailed in affluent families among the delightful valleys of Switzerland, even recur to my memory.[23]

This looks as if Mary had visited the household at Steventon and formed a firm opinion of their ménage. Why does she compare them to families in Switzerland? Did Mary travel there in her youth and experience a more open way of living – a more 'liberal society' – than was customary in England? As the daughter of the Master of Balliol, brought up in the hot house environment of Oxford, Mary had enjoyed an unusual upbringing and the opportunity to meet many of the wits and thinkers at the university and perhaps had a more enquiring mind than some of her contemporaries.

In Mary Shelley's *Frankenstein* written a generation later in 1818, the heroine Elizabeth writes warmly of Swiss society and its egalitarian nature:

The republican institutions of our country have produced simpler and happier manners than those which prevail in the great monarchies that surround it. Hence there is less distinction between the several classes of its inhabitants; and the lower orders…[24]

Mary Leigh's observations on the family are intriguing and chime, in some respects, with the mean-spirited remarks made in 1869 by one of Jane Austen's nieces, Fanny, bought up in the rich household of Edward Austen Knight at Godmersham and later married into the aristocratic Knatchbull family:

…it is very true that Aunt Jane from various circumstances was not so refined as she ought to have been from her talent…The [Austens] were not rich & the people around with whom they chiefly mixed, were not all high-bred, or in short anything more than mediocre & they of course tho' superior in mental powers & cultivation were on the same level as far as refinement goes...both the Aunts [Cassandra and Jane] were brought up in the most complete ignorance of the World and its ways (I mean as to fashion &c) & if it had not been for Papa's marriage [Edward Austen Knight] which brought them into Kent...they would have been... very much below par as to good Society & its ways.[25]

Mary Leigh was more generous in her appraisal of the Austen family seeing their lack of 'refinement' as a positive quality – 'simplicity of hospitality and taste'.

Claire Tomalin, a perceptive biographer of Jane Austen, commented on Fanny's put-down, looking at Jane's experiences within her elevated brother's house:

For an author who took social discomfort as one of her main themes, it meant that Godmersham was precious as a place in which to observe and record...No one observes the manners of a higher social class with more fascination that the person who feels they do not quite belong within the magic circle.[26]

Only at the end of Mary's history do we find any information on the author herself as she was too modest to provide any. It was penned by her husband, presumably after her death:

But of herself some just account shd be added by her surviving husband... She wrote some novels highly moral & entertaining. But her favourite amusement was drawing and painting in miniature...the withdrawing room at the Parsonage was hung with her paintings, as was likewise her dressing room with a paper of Chinese landscape all of her composition and painting. ... one of the most affectionate of wives & most agreeable cheerful and entertaining of companions.[27]

Perhaps these 'moral and entertaining novels' were circulated among the family as was common – it was certainly a habit in the Austen household as we know from Jane's letters. Her own novels were read aloud by the flickering of the fire and candles in the evenings before they were published and later her favourite niece, Anna would send her own work to Chawton for the family to read and discuss. Caroline Austen fondly recalled her Aunt Jane entertaining the family:

> She was considered to read aloud remarkably well. I did not often hear her but once I knew her take up a volume of Evelina and read a few pages of Mr. Smith and the Brangtons and I thought it was like a play. She had a very good speaking voice—this was the opinion of her contemporaries—and though I did not then think of it as a perfection, or ever hear it observed upon, yet its tones have never been forgotten—I can recall them even now—and I know they were very pleasant.[28]

I cannot imagine after reading the family history that Mary's novels were not entertaining and it is a pity that nothing of them survives.

Elizabeth Leigh

Jane Austen's other hostess during her stays at Adlestrop rectory was Elizabeth Leigh, the elder sister of the Revd Thomas and godmother to Jane's sister, Cassandra. Her name rarely appears in family trees or is noticed by the biographers of Jane Austen, but from Jane's letters it can be seen that Elizabeth was in frequent touch with the Austens and she was important in the chain of communication between the Austen-Leigh network of cousins. The Austens' letters are always directed to the inhabitants of the rectory rather than to their grander relations at Adlestrop Park.

Elizabeth never married and did not live with her brother and Mary until 1788. Her presence at the parsonage was noted by their neighbour Agnes Witts in her diary:

Tuesday Feb 10th 1789
...dropped Mr Witts at Chip:& went to Adlestrop to make a visit to Mrs Thos Leigh, more agreable than usual by the addition of Mrs Elizabeth Leigh, a very chearfull pleasant old maid[29]

Elizabeth remained a spinster perhaps because she spent some years looking after an elderly aunt, Elizabeth Wentworth, in Hendon or as Mary Leigh puts it 'rocking the reposing cradle of Mrs Wentworth's great age'. When Mrs Wentworth died at ninety-two she divided her 'affluent property' between her nephew, Revd Thomas and niece, Elizabeth. During her lifetime she had supported her other nephew, James Leigh, helping him to rebuild a part of the front of Adlestrop Park and giving him a sum 'sufficient to build two farmhouses' – perhaps Fern Farm and Hillside Farm (formerly called Parsonage Farm) which lie just outside the heart of the village on the western side.

The largest marble memorial tablet in Adlestrop Church is to Elizabeth Wentworth and recognises her benevolence to the Adlestrop Leighs – you can see it behind the pulpit. This lady not only had a pivotal role to play in the prosperity of the Leigh family but her own romantic story may have sown the seed of a plot theme for *Persuasion*.

Who was she exactly? Her maiden name was Elizabeth Lord and she was, as noted, the aunt of James, Thomas, Cassandra and Elizabeth Leigh – their mother's sister. The sisters' mother, a strong-willed widow, Rachel Lord was adamant that the two heiresses should both make an advantageous match and, when Elizabeth fell in love with a lowly Lieutenant Wentworth with no fortune to his name, Rachel vetoed his proposal. Daringly, the two lovers married in secret in 1720, before the dashing suitor departed with his regiment to France. When Rachel Lord discovered the deception she threatened to cut Elizabeth off and leave everything to Mary.

Returning from the wars with money and rank – now as Lieutenant-General Wentworth – William and Mary Leigh introduced their brother-in-law to Rachel under an assumed name and this time round she was charmed. The secret came out and Elizabeth was forgiven.[30] The Wentworths long loyalty to each other, despite family disapproval, remind Jane Austen's readers of Anne Elliott and her Captain Wentworth. The couple's happiness was cut short with the Lieutenant-General's death in 1747 at Turin, where he had been sent as British envoy. Elizabeth 'survived her husband 41 years and having no issue, proved a second parent to the children of her excellent sister and brother-in-law Wm and Mary Leigh'.

No romance brightened Elizabeth Leigh's life, her inheritance came too late to encourage any marriage prospects, although Jane always refers to her as Mrs E. Leigh – the Mrs was purely a mark of respect due to her age. The initial 'E' distinguishes her from 'Mrs Leigh' – the Hon. Mary Leigh of Stoneleigh Abbey – also mentioned in the collected letters. Elizabeth became a permanent companion to her younger brother after his wife died in 1797 both at Adlestrop and Stoneleigh and would have welcomed the Austens in their two later visits to the rectory.

Sometimes Jane just mentions as an aside in a letter to Cassandra: 'I have written to Mrs E. Leigh too...' – without specifying why but perhaps to save Cassandra the trouble of doing so.[31] In 1799 Jane is obviously trying to avoid a visit to Adlestrop as she writes to Cassandra from Bath:

I wonder what we shall do with all our intended visits this summer?—I should like to make a compromise with

Adlestrop, Harden [or Harpsden home of her cousin and rector, Edward Cooper] & Bookham [home of Samuel Cooke, also rector and Jane's godfather] that Martha's spending the summer at Steventon should be considered as our respective visits to them all.[32]

Rather than getting news direct from the family at Adlestrop Park it seems to always come via Elizabeth: 'My Mother has heard from Mrs E. Leigh—Lady S & S- and her daughter are going to remove to Bath.'[33] This refers to Lady Saye & Sele and her wild and divorced daughter, Mary-Cassandra Twisleton, Julia's sister – of whom more later.

When all the difficulties of the Stoneleigh inheritance were in full swing she makes a point of telling Cassandra, 'Mrs E.Leigh did not make the slightest allusion to my Uncle's Business as I remember telling you at the time but you shall hear it as often as you like. My Mother wrote to her a week ago.'[34]

In her mid-eighties Elizabeth fell ill and Jane was quick to send news of this to Cassandra with all the close detail that the sisters liked to exchange:

This post bought me two very interesting Letters, Yours & one from Bookham, in answer to an enquiry of mine about your good Godmother, of whom we had lately received a very alarming account from Paragon. Miss Arnold was the Informant there, & she spoke of Mrs E.L.'s having been very dangerously ill & attended by a physician from Oxford.—Your Letter to Adlestrop may perhaps bring you information from the spot, but in case it should not, I must tell you that she is better, tho' Dr Bourne cannot yet call her out of danger.

It is interesting that Elizabeth is still at Adlestrop Rectory at this time rather than at Stoneleigh. Jane goes on to more particulars:

Her disorder is an Inflammation on the Lungs, arising from a severe Chill, taken in Church last Sunday three weeks;–her Mind, all pious Composure, as may be supposed.–George Cooke was there when her Illness began, his Brother has now taken his place.–Her age & feebleness considered, one's fear cannot but preponderate–tho' her amendment has already surpassed the expectation of her Physician.

She adds a further titbit of news about Elizabeth's maidservant, Rebekah Cadwallader, 'I am sorry to add that Becky is laid up with a complaint of the same kind'. In the same long letter – written over the course of two days from Southampton – Jane ends by adding: 'As we have no letter from Adlestrop, we may suppose the good Woman was alive on Monday, but I cannot help expecting bad news from thence or Bookham, in a few days.'[35]

Two weeks later she writes with happy tidings of Elizabeth's recovery:

'She, good Woman, is I hope destined for some further placid enjoyment of her own Excellence in this World, for her recovery advances exceedingly well.—I had this pleasant news from Bookham last Thursday.'[36].

A few days later she remarks: 'Mrs E.L. is so much recovered as to get into the Dressing-room every day.'[37]

In fact Elizabeth did not die until she was ninety-three. Jane wrote to her niece, Caroline Austen on this occasion:

The note to your Papa, is to announce the death of that excellent woman Mrs Elizth Leigh; it came this morning enclosed in a Letter to Aunt Cassandra.—We all feel that we have lost a most valued old freind [sic], but the death of a person at her advanced age, so fit to die, & by her own feelings so ready to die, is not to be regretted.—She has been so kind as to leave a little remembrance £20 — to your Grandmama.[38]

In fact, it is rare that Jane spoke so warmly about her relations but every time she mentions Elizabeth it is to point out her goodness, her excellence and her value as an old friend. Elizabeth is buried in Adlestrop Church in the family vault adjoining her brother and his wife. The tablet on the south of the chancel simply states 'Elizabeth Leigh daughter of William Leigh born 17 November 1733 died 18 April 1816'.

Elizabeth outlived both her brothers, James and Thomas. After Thomas' death in 1813 she left Stoneleigh and returned to the rectory while James Henry and Julia took over the abbey. But before we turn our attention there we should go back a little to James Leigh in the forthcoming chapter and his tenure at Adlestrop Park. The history of his changes to the house and garden must have been very familiar to Jane Austen's mother and are important in appreciating the drive towards major improvements to the Leigh estate. Some of the changes that are described will ring a bell for any reader of *Mansfield Park*.

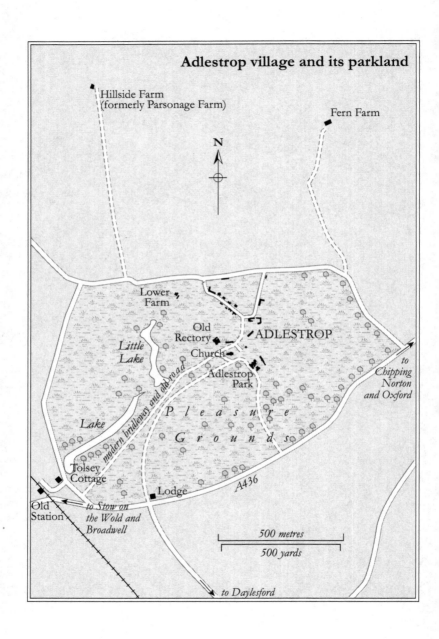

CHAPTER THREE

The Improving of Adlestrop Park

'...*James Leigh esq.; the present lord of the manor of Adlestrop. He married Caroline the only daughter of his grace the late duke of Chandois. He hath greatly repaired and enlarged the old family seat, in the Gothick taste, and resides here.*' **A New History of Gloucestershire, Samuel Ruddall, 1779**

James Leigh

James Leigh's inheritance of Adlestrop Park was assured once his father had cleared the family debts. William III and his wife had returned from Holland with their heir after their economical living abroad had saved the Adlestrop estate. The boy was first sent to Oxford to attend school staying with his uncle, Dr Theophilus Leigh II during the term, then he went to Westminster School and Malvern College, going up to Oxford as a gentleman commoner at Balliol College in 1740. Certainly he would have been a well-educated young man. Mary Leigh was only six years older than him and knew him from boyhood so naturally she sang his praises to his son:

he happily blended his Father's exuberant generosity, with his Mother's prudent economy...he divided his time between Adlestrop & his friends and though a fine young man of the world (in its best most sober sense); he always thought it worthwhile to be pleasant, cheerful & easy at

home; mingling readily with the old-fashioned mirth &
cheerfulness of Adlestrop.[1]

It is interesting how she characterises the village as 'old-
fashioned' – presumably comparing it to the brighter lights of
Oxford.

Following in his grandfather's footsteps and keeping to the
family tradition of marrying a well-connected cousin, James
Leigh chose Lady Caroline Brydges, the eldest daughter of the
second Duke of Chandos, Marquess of Carnarvon.

Despite his rank the duke was marked down by King
George II as a 'hot-headed, passionate, half-witted coxcomb'.
His daughter appears to have inherited none of his faults.

James, like his younger brother, was infected with the spirit
of the age – the wish to embellish and improve his lands and house. He not only embarked on much rebuilding of Adlestrop Park and remodelling of its garden but was also instrumental in repairing the church and changing

'…a park, a real park five miles round, a spacious modern-built house, so well placed and well screened as to deserve to be in any collection of engravings of gentlemen's seats in the kingdom.'
Mansfield Park

the lay-out of the land around it.

He was obviously prosperous enough to meet these costs
– although he had some financial help, as shown in Chapter
Two, from his rich aunt, Mrs Wentworth. The details of these
considerable upheavals and alterations are in the next chapter.
Mary Leigh has the best and most concise account of her
brother-in-law's achievements:

Upon Mr Leigh taking possession of Adlestrop, finding
the old park of his House beyond repair, he determined
to pursue the plan chalked out (by that celebrated genius,
and most worthy friend Mr Miller of Radway) upon Mrs

Wentworth first erection of the new Rooms. Removing therefore (& continuing near five years) into the then unoccupied Parsonage [this must have been during Dr Theophilus Leigh's incumbency], he deliberately executed his design & that in an excellent manner blending the useful with the elegant, for he was a man of business and entered into the minutiae of everything (both for himself and others) in which he was concerned.[2]

It is thanks to James and his choice of Sanderson Miller as an architect that the exquisite southwest frontage of Adlestrop Park was erected and, although his own son uprooted his cherished garden, this at least remains as a suitable epitaph to his vision and taste. His son's birth and his own demise are neatly encapsulated in Mary Leigh's vivid description:

The family were hardly disengaged from entertaining their numerous friends who came to admire & enjoy the renovated place, when on Feb 8th 1765 the only (long wished for) piece of furniture wanted, appeared in the Baby form of that James Henry Leigh of whom I have the honour of addressing. From the death of the Marchioness of Carnavon in July 1770, Lady Caroline and Mr Leigh spent the greatest part of their time with Lord Carnavon & it was at his house in Town, March 29th 1774, that by an almost sudden seizure you were bereaved of an excellent Father. ... just returned from finishing some disagreeable business in the City & expressing his joy on having accomplished it; when he was seized with a sudden spasm of his breath.[3]

The sudden and dramatic nature of James' death at the age of forty-nine, leaving a son and heir under the age of ten and a widow must have been a shock to his siblings at Adlestrop Rectory and the villagers, who on hearing the news would have wondered what it would mean for them. Any change at

Adlestrop Park would have repercussions for the whole area.

James was duly buried in the Leigh Vault in Adlestrop church and an elegant marble memorial to him shows a graceful lady leaning against an urn on the right side of the chancel arch which Jane must have admired in its pristine state. The tablet has all the usual encomiums to the deceased ending with the words: '... enemy to the licentiousness of the times, his zeal for religion, this church which he chiefly rebuilt, and its worship which he constantly attended.'

'In a Purse in Mr Leigh's pocket, four guineas and a half in gold and thirty-three shillings and sixpence in silver £6.8s.6d'
from Lady Caroline's notebook

A small ivory-covered notebook resides in the archives[4] and is described as belonging to Lady Caroline Leigh; in it she details assets found after her husband's death – even including the money in his pockets at the time. The stock and bank assets are listed, the payments for mourning clothes, the wages and the bills to the apothecary. It is a poignant reminder of all the duties that as a widow she had to undergo and how resourceful she was during her bereavement. Then, as now, lawyers, land agents and taxmen demanded information on the affairs of the deceased. There are details of legacies in his will which include £50 for the poor at Longborough and Adlestrop which was given to the Revd Thomas Leigh to distribute. It also notes that £4 was paid for the poor in Adlestrop from New Year's Day to Lady's Day Last.

Immediately after James' death a total inventory of all the contents of Adlestrop Park was made, room by room, the total being valued at £975.8s.8d.[5] Everything was included in every part of the establishment:

'...Green garret, steward's room, Maid's room, Nursery... in the tapestry chamber, best drawing room, closets, the Great Parlour, butler's pantry, servants hall and shoe room, housekeeping room, larder, kitchen store room, cellar and court, small beer cellar, laundry malt house, brewhouse, dairy chamber, dairy, gardener's room, stables, coach houses, coalhouse, yards, gardens, New Barn & Hovel, Lower Stables'[6]

All of the furniture, every paintings, each plate of china, glasses and linen were carefully itemised and valued. There was a list of the cellar's contents which included a hogshead of beer, dozens of bottles of Red Port, Cypress wine, old Madeira, Sack and Hock. Some of this was put up for sale but twenty-three hampers were sent to the Duke of Chandos' country house. Lady Caroline then moved out of Adlestrop to live with her brother, the third duke, in his town and country mansions, taking her son with her. This may have been to economise thereby keeping the estate intact for her son, or simply because she did not enjoy the seclusion of the country without her husband.

'...the house, and grounds, and furniture, were approved...terms, time, everything...'
Persuasion

Adlestrop Park was then let, first to a Mr Thomas Drake and then later, in 1778 a lease was drawn up with Joseph Sabin to rent it plus its grounds and lands, fully furnished on a yearly tenancy of £84 for the house and grounds, plus £35.18s for lands. On this document Lady Caroline Leigh and Revd Thomas Leigh are shown as James Henry Leigh's guardians,[7] although Mary Leigh believes that the Duke of Chandos also shared in this role. The Revd Thomas Leigh, always the family workhorse, took over all the administration of the Leigh business at Adlestrop and went about his own improvements at the rectory waiting, no doubt, impatiently for his nephew to come of age and take up the family baton again.

'Adlestrop House was let & every prudent step was taken... of which now you reap the fruits gathered in Minority[8]'.

James Henry Leigh

He was first educated at Odiham School in Hampshire before boarding at Winchester school. Both these schools were close to the magnificent Palladian mansion of Avington Park, the ducal country seat where Lady Caroline and her brother preferred to live. It is also very near to the Austen's stamping ground at Steventon but there is no evidence that there were visits between these cousins whereas the connection between the Leighs and the Chandos family continued for many years. In 1812, Lady Caroline's niece wrote in a letter to a friend: 'All the Leighs have been here till yesterday when they returned to Adlestrop where I hope (please God) to join them & spend some days there.'

When he was an undergraduate at Christchurch College, Oxford, James Henry and his mother spent the long summer holiday in Adlestrop to introduce him 'by degrees into the great world and to familiarise him to his country neighbours...upon his coming of age (and spent most hospitably and celebrated here) Adlestrop became his chief residence'.[9]

It must have been a definite shock to the system for the Leighs to return to Adlestrop Park, a house considerably smaller and far less grandiose than the ducal residences. It is probable that James Henry's closeness to his mother's family gave him great confidence and perhaps a touch of hauteur. Like a true hero, he was to fall violently in love at first sight with his cousin, the teenage daughter of Lord Saye & Sele, Julia Judith Twisleton (1771-1843) who was staying with her parents at Adlestrop rectory: '...On entering – he was instantaneously shot! – shot in a vital part by the mischievous wicked eyes of his fair cousin – the Sorceress was not quite fiveteen.'[10]

James Henry wrote a wildly enthusiastic letter in his flowing hand to his mother from Broughton Castle on 20 October 1786:

Madam

I have the pleasure to inform you that Miss Twisleton Ld. Saye & Sele's eldest daughter has done me the greatest honor by accepting my proposal of marriage & I must hope it will meet with your intire approbation.[11]

The Revd would have been delighted too as Miss Twisleton was his great-niece whom he would have known since her infancy. Mary Leigh describes their wedding in 1786 at Broughton Castle, near Banbury in Oxfordshire (about twelve miles from Adlestrop) and the family seat of the Saye & Seles as 'quite a Richardsonian Wedding'.[12]

This aside would have interested Jane as she adored the works of Samuel Richardson and had almost learnt *Sir Charles Grandison* off by heart according to her nephew, James Edward Austen-Leigh in his *Memoir*, and even went so far as to remind her family of Sir Charles' wedding anniversary on the appropriate day.[13]

Broughton Castle was described by Sir Charles Oman in the nineteenth century as 'about the most beautiful castle in all England…for sheer loveliness of the combination of water, woods and picturesque buildings'. Julia was very young to be married or even to be 'out' in society but her husband was only six years older than her and, at the time, marrying at an early age was a cause for celebration rather than censure. Look at Mrs Bennet's sense of pride when Lydia is to be married – despite the scandalous circumstances of her elopement with Wickham: 'Well! I am so happy. In a short time I will have a daughter married. Mrs Wickham! How well it sounds. And she was only sixteen last June.'

It was through the Leighs that Jane would have become familiar with the Twisletons – who can only be described as a dysfunctional family. The Revd Thomas' other sister, Cassandra, had married Sir Edward Turner of Ambrosden and their eldest daughter, Elizabeth, was to marry Thomas

Twisleton, the 13th Lord Saye & Sele – hence the connection between the two families. At Broughton Castle in the long Gothick gallery are three paintings of great interest. Two are Gainsborough portraits of Elizabeth and her husband, the 13th Lord – Elizabeth's portrait shows a dark-haired charming young woman while her ruddy faced husband has a solid expression under his wig. In between them is hung a large ensemble painting of the Leigh and Turner families featuring Sir Edward and Lady Turner, William Leigh of 'Addlestrop' in a wig and three woman whose identities are not certain and seem to be wrongly identified by the lettering at the base. The central figure of Lady Turner (née Cassandra Leigh) is seated and holds a lattice basket of peaches in her lap and she offers one of them to Sir Edward. They were married in 1739 and although the painting is currently dated to around 1735, a slightly later date would fit if it was, as it seems to be, a painting celebrating their marriage. Presumably their daughter brought the painting to her new home at Broughton, proud of her heritage. Her own marriage was to end in a most tragic fashion when her husband, Lord Saye & Sele, a hero of the British army for his leadership in quelling the Gordon Riots in 1780, committed suicide just two years after his daughter's wedding.[14]

The eccentricity of these Leigh and Austen cousins does not stop there – Julia's elder brother, Thomas, adored amateur dramatics and when he appeared in a private production, also by coincidence a play titled *Julia*, he was cast opposite a young lady noted for her beauty, a Miss Charlotte Wattell. A few months afterwards the couple eloped, (he was still a schoolboy) and married at Gretna Green. Thomas Twisleton still gained his BA and MA degrees at Oxford and was ordained. He became an absentee rector of the Adlestrop and Broadwell livings and ended his bizarre career as Archbishop of Colombo, Sri Lanka where he died in 1824.[15] Perhaps the knowledge of these two Julias subconsciously suggested the name of Julia Bertram in *Mansfield Park* – a thoughtless and headstrong young woman who also eloped to Scotland. We know Jane took a keen interest in this family because in May 1801 she wrote to Cassandra about Julia's notorious younger sister, Mary-Cassandra. Mary-Cassandra had first eloped in 1790 (encouraged by her brother's example perhaps) to marry Edward-Jervis Ricketts by whom she had three children, he then divorced her after she had committed adultery in 1797 with an MP at his house in London. It must have caused a great scandal at the time. Jane spotted her at a ball in Bath, remarking (not in a kind way) on her resemblance to Mrs Leigh – meaning Julia Leigh of Adlestrop:

> I then got Mr Evelyn to talk to, & Miss Twisleton to look at; and I am proud to say that I have a very good eye at an Adultress, for tho' repeatedly assured that another in the same party was the She, I fixed upon the right one from the first.—A resemblance to Mrs Leigh was my guide. She is not so pretty as I expected; her face has the same defect of baldness as her sister's, and her features not so handsome;—she was highly rouged, & looked rather quietly and contentedly silly than anything else.[16]

Jane Austen had obviously observed Mrs Leigh closely after trips to Adlestrop. Julia must have been proud of her lineage and by all accounts, she, like her mother, became a redoubtable woman who was to provoke quite strong reactions amongst the Austens. When the Austens were at Adlestrop Rectory James Henry Leigh would have been ensconced a stone's throw away at the Park with his young wife who may have been rather condescending towards the Austens and their lack of wealth and pretension. As a married woman Julia, although only four years older than Jane, would have looked down her nose at the two spinsters without a penny to their names. Did the Austens experience an occasion that mirrored Elizabeth Bennet's first dinner with Mr Collins' formidable patron, Lady Catherine

'Lady Catherine was a tall, large woman, with strongly marked features, which might once have been handsome. Her air was not conciliating, nor was her manner of receiving them such as to make her visitors forget their inferior rank.'
Pride and Prejudice

de Bourg at Rosings Park – so amusingly exaggerated in *Pride and Prejudice?*

Another more likeable side to the newlyweds was how they kept their house full of visitors and entertained the neighbourhood. In an exceptional cold and icy January in 1789 they cheered their friends and themselves up with amateur dramatics on three separate evenings where plays were performed on a makeshift stage in their drawing room with seats for an invited audience including their house party guests. The first play chosen early in the month was *Matilda* which was also a play that Jane Austen's elder brothers performed at Christmas in 1782 at Steventon when Jane was only seven. They used an old barn near to the house

'…a love of the theatre is so general, an itch for acting so strong among young people, that he could hardly out-talk the interest of his hearers. From the first casting of the parts, to the epilogue, it was all bewitching'
Mansfield Park

and the tradition was carried on for the next few years while James was still at home. Perhaps the contrivances for staging a play at Adlestrop by converting the drawing room into a mock theatre were nearer to the ploys that Henry Crawford had to improvise at Mansfield Park where the billiard room was used instead and Mrs Norris has to make a stage curtain from 'an enormous roll of green baize.'

Adlestrop's theatrical evenings sound amusing and diverting as Agnes Witts who lived in Swerford Park, near Chipping Norton, recalled in her diary on two separate occasions in January 1789:

...dining early to go to the Play at Adlestrop, with which we were far more entertain'd than expected...the Drawing Room made a tolerable good Theatre tho' the stage was too small: 24 Spectators out of the Neighbourhood.[17]

Wensday Jan 21st
...we early went to the play at Adlestrop Venice Preserved & who is the Dupe [A restoration play by Thomas Otway], with a Prologue between by Mr Oliphant in the character of Mother Shipton riding on a Broomstick, Mr Twisleton was very great in Pierre and Mr Leigh little less so in Jaffier. Mrs Twisleton was not equal to Belvederes difficult part, the Theatre was very full & we did not get home till past two[18]

Nine months later on a hot day in August the Witts went to dinner at the Park having entertained Mr Leigh, his aunt Elizabeth and Miss Twisleton(Mrs Leigh was not well enough to come) at their house two days earlier:

Wensday Aug 12th
...we were almost broil'd going in the two Post Chaises to Dine at Mr Leighs at Adlestrop, first making a short visit to the Parsonage, sat down 11 to Dinner, rather formal but Mrs Leigh is always pleasant & agreeable not at home until quite late.[19]

Both at Adlestrop Park and later at Stoneleigh Abbey Julia instigated huge improvements to the interiors spending enormous sums of money. Her son and heir, Chandos Leigh was born in Harley Street in 1791 and Jane might even have played with him as a toddler. According to her grandson, Edward, Julia was 'inclined to be too managing' and both her husband and children lived in some fear of her disapproval.[20] James Henry was a politician and a Member of Parliament from 1802 until 1823. He first represented the constituencies of Marlborough and Great Bedwyn both under the control of his kinsman, the earl of Ailesbury and then from 1818 until his death, he was the member for Winchester in the interest of his cousin, the Marquess of Buckingham.[21] This was before the Reform Act of 1832 when the Rotten Borough of Great Bedwyn, for example, was among many to be abolished. Rotten Boroughs and Pocket Boroughs were controlled by peers, who gave their seats to their relatives or friends, to ensure landed interests were protected in the House of Commons. A major landowner had huge power over his constituent tenants as, at this time, there was no secret ballot.

It was a system remarkably similar to the giving of livings in the Church of England – both depending often on family patronage without necessarily expecting the holder of the role to actually work on behalf of either their parishioners or constituents.

CHAPTER FOUR

An Eighteenth-century Village: the Adlestrop that Jane Austen first knew

'...*at length the Parsonage was discernible. The garden sloping to the road, the house standing it in, the green pales and the laurel hedge, every thing declared they were arriving...*' **Pride and Prejudice**

It is easy to imagine Jane as a fresh-faced teenager with her sister, Cassandra, aged twenty-one looking eagerly out of the windows of their conveyance as their mother, well into middle age, pointed out to them fondly remembered landmarks along the road to Adlestrop. The family could enjoy the advantages of new, comparatively comfortable sprung carriages on the smooth surface of the turnpike roads to make their cross-country journey.

It was during Jane's lifetime that widespread travelling for leisure became possible thanks to the turnpike road system and the availability of roadworthy carriages. The Austens in common with other middle class families kept their own carriage at Steventon which would have been drawn by either two or four horses. In his memoir, James Edward

'But what is distance, Mr Weston, to people of large fortune? — you would be amazed to hear how my brother, Mr Suckling, sometimes flies about. You will hardly believe me — but twice in one week he and Mr. Bragge went to London and back again with four horses' *Emma*

Austen-Leigh refers to it: 'A carriage and pair of horses was kept... once bought [it] entailed little further expense; and the horses... were often employed on farm work.'[1] Just like the Leighs and the Bennets.

The Austens seldom used their carriage for long journeys but those who had superior horses would have travelled the first part of the journey, say twenty miles, before changing to fresh ones at posting inns en route. Otherwise the horses would rest overnight or just for a couple of hours, as General Tilney allows for the chaise and four at the Petty France Inn between Bath and Northanger. A tedious wait 'in which there was nothing to be done but eat without being hungry, and loiter about without anything to see'.[2]

There were two main ways of travelling – by stage coach or by a hired post-chaise drawn by either two or four hired horses. Stage coaches were not considered quite the thing for ladies to travel in and so the Austens may have chosen the more expensive option of the post-chaise. Jane often had to fit in with her brothers' plans if she wished to travel as they were needed to accompany her – although she did occasionally journey alone.

In September 1796 Jane wrote to Cassandra: 'As to the mode of our Travelling to Town—*I* want to go in a Stage Coach, but Frank will not let me.'[3] The more respectable and more costly post-chaises were painted yellow and had the nickname of 'yellow bounders'; they could seat between two to four passengers inside with one perhaps sitting outside alongside the postilion. Both would have used the countrywide network of 'stages' and coaching inns for changing horses and taking their meals or when they needed an overnight stay.

Outside the quiet village of Steventon there were two coaching inns within a mile or so of the vicarage: the Deane Gate Inn where the local road joined the turnpike on the coach route to Andover and Basingstoke and the Wheatsheaf on the well-travelled Winchester to Basingstoke road off Popham

Lane where coaches stopped for Alton just a short distance from Steventon.

At Alton they would change coaches at the Swan for Southampton where coaches and chaises could be found for London. The coaching inns were not only used for travel, but for the embryonic postal system of the time, so the Austens would pick up and pay for their letters at either place or leave them for posting.

From Hampshire to Adlestrop would have taken a minimum of ten to twelve hours, if one calculates a carriage going at about seven miles an hour, and it is likely they would stop overnight – perhaps at Oxford if they took a direct route. When the Austens came to Adlestrop in 1806 they were journeying from Southampton and travelled via Clifton in Bristol and Cheltenham. Cheltenham, like Bath, was a fashionable spa resort. Eliza de Feuillide stayed there in 1797 and complained that the journey was uncomfortable during the last few stages 'as we had a drunken Post Boy, and some very steep hills to ascend and descend...'[4] A good description of travelling through the hilly Cotswolds. She elaborated:

> The place is very full, and I have met with many of my acquaintance among the rest some relations of my Aunt Austen, that is to say Mr. & Mrs. Leigh, and Lord & Lady Say & Sele...There are Plays three times a week...and Balls twice[5]

It is possible the Austens also went via Bristol on their earlier trips as Jane was quite familiar with both Devizes (where the coach may have stopped to change horses, probably at the Bear Inn) and Bristol and its surrounding countryside. Bristol and its rolling downs are referred to in a piece of juvenalia, *Lesley Castle*, penned in 1792, and in *Northanger Abbey* the oafish John Thorpe tries to persuade Catherine Morland to join him on a jaunt to Bristol from Bath taking in the mock-Gothic Blaise

'An easy distance do you call it?
It is nearly fifty miles.'
'And what is fifty miles of good
road? Little more than half a
day's journey. Yes, I call it a very
easy distance'
Pride and Prejudice

Castle and the Vanbrugh house at Kingsweston which demonstrate Jane Austen's knowledge of the region.

There are many references to travelling in the novels culminating in poor Catherine Morland's flight from the wrath of General Tilney on 'a journey of seventy miles to be taken post by you, at your age alone, unattended!'. She set off at seven in the morning in the Tilney carriage to be taken to Salisbury, the first stage of her trip home at Fullerton, there she had to rely upon the post-masters 'for the names of the places which were then to conduct her'. Luckily she met with no misadventures 'and stopping only to change horses' reached her destination between six and seven in the evening – a long journey of eleven hours; an ordeal that the Austens would have certainly avoided.

Adlestrop is not far north from the old Cotswold Ridgeway which ran from Northampton and crossed the Fosse Way at Stow on the Wold. The historian Leland used this road in Henry VIII's reign and noted 'Adlesthorp and Horse Bridge' about halfway between Stow and Chipping Norton. That 'Horse Bridge' would have been very near the present one over the main railway line. In the sixteenth century the main road lay within the village near to the church but by the mid-eighteenth century it had moved to follow the steepest part of the ridge some 200 yards south of the church – this can be clearly seen on the old maps. In 1755 the present A436 which skirts the village was designated a toll road that connected the turning to Chipping Norton, from the old pub called the Cross Hands (now the Greedy Goose restaurant) to Stow on the Wold. Coming into Stow up the long hill from Adlestrop, you can see Pike Cottage opposite to the Bell Inn where tolls were paid. The Turnpike Trusts were each responsible for a stretch of road, usually a length of twenty miles, for a fixed time such as twenty-one years. Their jurisdiction was finally ended by Parliament in 1870. The toll roads were called turnpikes because the toll gate had a row of pikes along their top rail which, if necessary, could be turned to face the oncoming traffic to deter anyone attempting to dodge paying the fee.

At the side road to Adlestrop, just by Leland's 'Horse Bridge', there was a turnpike gate by Tolsey cottage. The house still stands today, although it has been greatly extended and refurbished over the centuries. In a dry summer the lanes would have been thick with the white limestone dust of the Cotswolds, thickly bordered by hedges of hawthorn, blackthorn, elderflower, willow herb, threaded by dog roses and the verges decorated with feathery white Queen Anne's lace. On the Austens' first visit in the 1790s their carriage would have taken them across the fields from where Jane and Cassandra would have been excited to glimpse

'When they left the high road for the lane to Hunsford, every eye was in search of the Parsonage, and every turning expected to bring it in view. The palings of Rosings Park was their boundary on one side... at length the Parsonage was discernible... In a moment they were all out of the chaise, rejoicing at the sight of each other.' *Pride and Prejudice*

the crocketed Gothic frontage of Adlestrop Park, the church tower on its knoll, continuing right up to the front door of the parsonage to be greeted by Mary Leigh and her husband, the rector. Their clothes, hats and luggage would have been covered in the fine powder thrown up by the horses' hooves and carriage wheels, which was known as pye powder after the French phrase 'pied poudré' – literally 'dusty feet'.

Steventon and Adlestrop were both rural communities and of similar size – although Steventon boasted two inns but

Adlestrop village has never had a licensed pub – whether this was a deliberate plan of the Leighs has never been determined. There is no record of the family itself ever leaning towards temperance – the cellars at Adlestrop Park were always well stocked. What would Jane have seen when she walked from the parsonage?

Many of the houses of the villagers would have been thatched, whereas now only one, the current post office, boasts a recently refurbished thatch. Other roofs, steeply pitched and gabled, were tiled with the traditional stone slates of the region. Some Cotswold quarries specialised in their production using the natural process of leaving stone exposed in the winter 'so that the moisture in the thin films of clay between the layers freezes, thus expanding the pendle, as it is called, so that it splits easily into slates'.[6] Each slate would be fastened onto wooden battens on the roofs with a wooden peg or nail bedded on moss, hay or straw. The tilers who laid these roofs were real artisans and some of their work, beautifully weathered over centuries, peppered with mosses and lichens, still survives. The cottages were constructed in the time-honoured vernacular style of the Cotswolds with thick walls of local stone and small or dormer windows on an upper storey or attic. Inside the stone was covered with wattle and daub and roughly plastered or faced with deal boards or just left plain – especially by a large fireplace. The floors would be stone flagged downstairs while upstairs they were laid with broad wooden planks, often made of elm. The front entrances opened straight into a downstairs room with a generous stone hearth and open fireplace of about six feet with stone jambs and a huge roughly cut wooden beam above it. Upstairs the bedrooms had low and sloping ceilings under their dormer roofs and were often overcrowded and unsanitary. Even in Elizabethan times the condition of cottagers was cause for concern and in 1589 an Act was passed whereby no cottage could be built without four acres of ground being assigned to it and no more than one family to live in it but, despite this forward thinking, cramped and rubble built houses persisted in rural pockets[7]. Most villagers had houses that were two up and two down and if you had a large family that meant a lot of bed-sharing and squalor. Although Cotswold cottages are now considered charming, in the eighteenth and nineteenth centuries they were regarded as dirty hovels.

In 1801, a few years after Jane's first visit to Adlestrop, there was a census and the statistics were all gathered by Thomas Leigh and recorded in his neat hand. The population of the village was considerably larger than it is now. A register headed 'Population and Poor's Rates of Slaughter Hundred April 1801' gives the statistics for 24 villages in the area starting with Adlestrop and finishing with Windrush.[8] In Adlestrop there were 38 houses, 116 males, 109 females making a total of 225 persons in all, slightly bigger than Steventon's 33 families while Jane's last home in Chawton had a population of 347 in 1811. The Revd Leigh kept a very careful record of the village population and of its marriages, christenings and burials from 1539 up to 1811 noting 'that we have always had more births than burials [and that] we are rather more populous now than we were 200 years ago[9].

Jane would have found no shops of interest in Adlestrop, nothing like a milliner or a circulating library, there was only a falling down water mill, a blacksmith's and a butcher's shop.[10] Thomas Barker, an earlier village butcher, was prosperous enough on his death in 1707 to leave annuities of 20 shillings to the poor of Adlestrop and also ten shillings each to the poor of Longborough and Evenlode. Presumably he took his stock on a cart to sell to those villages while basing himself in Adlestrop.

The villages in the novels resemble a settlement somewhere in between those of Adlestrop and Chawton. Highbury in *Emma* was the largest: 'almost amounting to a town'; it boasted an inn with post horses for hire, a drapery shop, a butcher's and baker's and even an opticians. Mrs Goddard kept a school for young ladies where three teachers worked. There were other professionals who lived and worked there such as the assiduous Mr Perry, an apothecary and a lawyer. Despite this Emma herself finds it a disappointment:

> Much could not be hoped from the traffic of even the busiest part of Highbury… her eyes fell only on the butcher with his tray, a tidy old woman travelling home with her full basket, two curs quarrelling over a dirty bone, and string of dawdling children round the baker's little low window, eyeing the gingerbread…

A perfect picture of provincial ennui. How much more of a backwater was Thornton Lacey, tucked away in rural fields, with only a farm and a blacksmith's forge and, apart from the parsonage, no other building that could be called a gentlemen's residence. In contrast Uppercross in *Persuasion* was a:

> moderate-sized village, which a few years back had been completely in the old English style, containing only two houses superior in appearance to those of the yeoman and labourers; the mansion of the squire with its high walls, great gates, and old trees, substantial and unmodernized, and the compact tight parsonage, enclosed in its own neat garden, with a vine and a peartree trained around its casements; but upon the marriage of the young squire, it had received the improvement of a farmhouse, elevated into a cottage, for his residence.

Uppercross Cottage had been made more upmarket by the addition of a verandah, French windows and 'other prettinesses'. Both Mansfield and Delaford have a butcher's shop but Henry Tilney's Woodston sounds a better bet and is described as a 'large and populous village' with a number of little chandler's shops and some neat houses 'above the rank of a cottage'. The surrounding countryside although 'in a situation not unpleasant' has the disadvantage of being flat.

It is illuminating how many fine distinctions Jane Austen's characters voice on what makes a village desirable and doubtless they would have found Adlestrop sadly wanting. But Jane would have found enjoyment in the traditional proximity of church, mansion and parsonage and delighted in the beauties of the countryside and the views of valleys and hills. There were also an extensive number of neighbouring 'good' families to socialise with who called at the parsonage.

In the ensuing ten years from 1 January 1801 to 1811 there were 15 marriages, 73 baptisms and 40 burials in Adlestrop and the population rose by an increase of 23. In 1900 the population had declined to 169 but the village still had shops, many carts coming and going selling and picking up goods and, of course, its famous railway station where Edward Thomas's train 'drew up there unwontedly.' In 2010 there are 37 houses, 32 males and 40 females making a total of 72 persons in all – almost two-thirds less than in Jane Austen's time. The number of houses is almost the same as in 1801 which shows how overcrowded some of the cottages must have been. Today there is a single shop combined with a post office and just one bus a week that stops a little way outside the village. The railway station was closed in 1966 and its infrastructure pulled down, although the tracks remain, and the Hereford–Worcester line still rattles through the ghost station on an intercity service to Paddington.

While now it is perfectly possible to walk through the village without seeing anyone in the street or in the surrounding fields, it would have been far livelier in the eighteenth century. Large families were normal and children would have played in the lanes, easily dodging the infrequent horses and carts and helping out on the farms, especially at harvest time, when they were old enough to do so. The village pump would have been a busy meeting place – only its wooden stump now remains outside Leigh Cottage halfway down Main Street. Mains water did not arrive in the village until 1928. It is likely that Adlestrop Park and the parsonage may have had their own wells to draw water from as there are numerous springs and streams in the vicinity.

As at Steventon, Adlestrop's main activity two hundred years ago was agriculture. Around the village crops were grown, cows grazed to be later milked by dairymaids, sheep were watched over by the village shepherd, horses kept for transporting goods, carriages, carts and for the inhabitants themselves to ride on. Oxen were kept for ploughing. Horses generated work for a blacksmith, stable lads and grooms, coachmen and carters. The upper echelons kept horses for their carriages, riding and hunting – a prime amusement – while the farmers needed them for transporting and moving heavy loads. In her *Family History*, Mary Leigh recounts how James Henry Leigh's grandparents, William III and Mary, managed their horses:

> 'It was Fanny's first ball, though without the preparation or splendour of many a young lady's first ball, being the thought only of the afternoon, built on the late acquisition of a violin player in the servants' hall...'
> *Mansfield Park*

> ...good Mrs Leigh never unnecessarily took off the four long tailed mares from the farm... and the greatest favour Mr Leigh could grant was lending his horses....whilst the young people borrowed or hired Village Steeds, on which, they scowered the Country. Dancing and the sound of Crowdero's Fiddle (for such a musician was the old blacksmith) always dismissed Mr Leigh early to bed for tho' he would not contradict his young ones, he never loved either Dancing or Musick'[11]

A blacksmith was a common trade and in Adlestrop the smithy was leased to a John Scolar in 1706 north-east of Manor Farm

– perhaps the famous fiddler. Today there is a smart house converted from an old barn still known as Smith's barn on Schooler's Lane which may have been on or near the site of this smithy and the name of the lane itself may come from Scolar. At harvest time and haymaking all available hands, men, women and children were employed to bring the crops of oats and corn in on a day rate and once there was a miller to grind the corn. Nearly all the local families would have worked on the land using their muscle and labour to do so.

The water-mill that had stood in Adlestrop northwest of Lower Farm since the twelfth century was demolished before 1799 having been in a state of dereliction for some years. Its semi-circular grooved grinding stone was saved and now functions as a solid step into the church. In 1732 the miller was noted as a Quaker.[12]

Jane was well acquainted with country ways and would have found Adlestrop's rural habits perfectly familiar; the contrast between the wants of the village and those accustomed to London life are beautifully pointed up when Mary Crawford wants her harp to be brought from Northampton to the parsonage at Mansfield:

'We heard tidings of my harp at last… it was seen by some farmer, and he told the miller, and the miller told the butcher, and the butcher's son-in-law left word at the shop.' *Mansfield Park*

> To want a horse and cart in the country seemed impossible, so I told my maid to speak for one directly; and as I cannot look out of my dressing-closet without seeing one farm yard, nor walk in the shrubbery without passing another, I thought it would be only to ask and have….guess my surprise, when I found I had been asking the most unreasonable, most impossible thing in the world, had offended all the farmers, all the labourers, all the hay in the parish.

Edmund replied:

> You could not be expected to have thought on the subject
> before, but when you do think of it, you must see the
> importance of getting in the grass. The hire of a cart at any
> time, might not be so easy as you suppose; our farmers are
> not in the habit of letting them out; but in harvest, it must
> be quite out of their power to spare a horse.[13]

In *Mansfield Park* Fanny, who rides a quiet mare every day
for the sake of her health is obliged to share her mount with
Mary Crawford to the detriment of her own well-being. At
Steventon Jane Austen's brothers certainly all rode but Jane and
Cassandra did not. The rectory at Steventon had about three
acres of glebe land on which they cultivated their vegetables
and Mr Austen rented the nearby 200-acre Cheesedown Farm
which produced all the family's meat and other crops for bread
and beer-making – wheat, barley, oats and hops.[14] This familiar
pattern was repeated in the rector's own large walled garden
and on his glebe land at Adlestrop.

To return to the census of 1801 we can see that 36 families
in all worked the land, 8 were in trade and 2 families that came
under neither heading and to this tally the Revd. Leigh also
added the household of James Henry Leigh who, at the time
of the census, resided in Harley Street, London. His extensive
household comprised a total of 20 persons: 7 male and 13
female. This number of people in a single household reflects
the high proportion of servants employed. Presumably many
of these would have travelled with the family to London.

Servants were on hand for the Leigh families in Adlestrop
Park and the rectory where there was linen to be washed and
laundered, beer to be brewed, gardens and pleasure grounds
to maintain. One of the outside cottages adjacent to the
mansion still carries the name of Laundry Cottage. As late as
the nineteen-thirties there were 26 staff at Adlestrop Park. This

information was gathered by local historian, Janet Walker, from Ivy Clifford who worked there as a housemaid.[15] The indoor staff consisted of a butler, cook, kitchen maid, scullery maid, head housemaid, second and third housemaid, a parlour maid who served at meals and waited on the family, the ladies maid and her assistant and two sewing maids who looked after and repaired the clothes and linen. All these servants lived in and their food and lodging were part of their wages. Three women from the village undertook the washing in the outside cottage and a village lad was the boot boy who polished the shoes and brought in coal and logs for the stoves and fires. Outdoors was a chauffeur and a lad to assist him, the gamekeeper also with a lad to help, the head gardener, second gardener and a garden lad, and a head groom, under groom and a stable lad.

Jane Austen would easily recognise most of the top end of Adlestrop with the juxtaposition of the church on its high ground overlooking the rectory which remains the pretty scene it must have always been, enhanced by lack of traffic. What was once the main road into the village across the park, is now a dead end leading to a quiet shaded bridleway threading its way between the dry stone walls of the park and the old rectory to a kissing gate. The old pleasure ground beyond boasts one of the most scenic cricket pitches in the country. When the weather is dry, the old track over which Jane's coach would have travelled can be clearly seen like a shadow on the manicured grass of the cricket ground.

The history of Adlestrop rectory and its grounds is uncannily like the long conversation Henry Crawford has with Edmund Bertram about the village of Thornton Lacey in *Mansfield Park*. Henry relates his previous day's adventures during a lull in the card game, Speculation, while he is seated around the table with his sister, Mary Crawford, Fanny Price and her visiting brother William, Lady Bertram and Edmund.

While out hunting Crawford discovered that his horse had lost a shoe so he was obliged to seek out another way home through the very place where Edmund is to live after his ordination: Thornton Lacey. Crawford describes its setting:

> I was suddenly, upon turning the corner of a steepish downy field, in the middle of a retired little village between gently rising hills; a small stream before me to be forded, a church stands on a sort of knoll to my right — which church was strikingly large and handsome for the place, and not a gentleman or half a gentleman's house to be seen excepting one — to be presumed the Parsonage, within a stone's throw of the said knoll and church.

In reply to Edmund asking him 'How did you like what you saw?' Henry at once starts talking about possible improvements to the building: 'Very much indeed. You are a lucky fellow. There will be work for five summers at least before the place is live-able.'

It is noteworthy that Henry Crawford sees that working on changing a house and landscape over a five-year period is an ideal way to pass one's time. Crawford elaborates his ideas:

> The farm-yard must be cleared away entirely, and planted up to shut out the blacksmith's shop. The house must be turned to front the east instead of the north — the entrance and principal rooms, I mean, must be on that side, where the view is really very pretty....you must make you a new garden at what is now the back of the house; which will be giving it the best aspect in the world...[16]

This turning of the house to make the most of the fine view of undulating ground exactly reflects what happened to Adlestrop Parsonage under the hand of the Revd Thomas Leigh, although the entrance was returned back to its current position in the nineteenth century and the obtrusive bays added, which perhaps spoil the original elegance and symmetry of the house.[17] The value of the Adlestrop church living in 1814 exactly mirrors the fictional living of Edmund's which was worth £700 a year. Jane Austen was a stickler for getting facts and figures correct.

Henry Crawford praises the house:

> I never saw a house of the kind which had in itself so much the air of a gentleman's residence, so much the look of something above a mere Parsonage House...it is a solid, roomy, mansion-like house, such as one might suppose a respectable old country family had lived in from generation to generation, through two centuries at least, and were now spending two to three thousand a year in.

The description given in *Northanger Abbey* on Woodston rectory where Henry Tilney lived has a similar ring:

> At the further end of the village, and tolerably disengaged from the rest of it, stood the parsonage, a new-built substantial stone house, with its semicircular sweep and green gates.

In Mary Leigh's history she records her husband's improvements to the house and its gardens from 1763 onwards:

> Dr Leigh resigned the Adlestrop Living and yr father James Leigh presenting it to his brother, Thomas Leigh, he immediately began a thorough repair of the Parsonage House, turning the entrance and main front westward, making there a new creation of a Pleasure Ground, by destroying a dirty farmyard & house which came within a few yards of the Windows. ..Upon the enclosure in the year 75, Blundels Field became allotted to the Parsonage, he further enlarged his garden laying near three acres of ground under Water in front of his house and passing to the Walks on its banks by turning an arch under the road.

Those improvements with the addition of kitchen gardens & offices render the Parsonage very compleat.[18]

Another hand has been added at the end of Mary's writing on the house: 'And long may it prove a fine provision for a younger son of the family!'

The significance of the improvements in 1775 show that long before Humphry Repton was to arrive on the scene, Revd Thomas had already added the Little Lake to his view, turned the entrance and got rid of the farm buildings – just as years later Jane's characters were to propose. Like her fictional vicars, Mr Collins and Mr Elton, it is reasonable to suppose that Jane's cousins would have given the Austens a full tour of their house and grounds, pointing out the views, the excellence of their garden and explaining carefully all the works that had been undertaken. It may have been tedious to hear but obviously some of it sank into Jane's consciousness. Although it was many years before she would write *Mansfield Park* – it is thought that she did not begin it until 1811 – the roots of one of its motifs could have sprung from her cousin's labours in Adlestrop.

'Here, leading the way through every walk and cross walk, and scarcely allowing them an interval to utter the praises he asked for, every view was pointed out with a minuteness which left beauty entirely behind. He could number the fields in every direction, and could tell how many trees there were in the most distant clump.'
Pride and Prejudice

After admiring the rectory and its new arrangements and its views down the sloping field to the little lake, the other house of much greater distinction was of course Adlestrop Park, literally a two minute walk away just behind the church. The alterations to both house and garden can be taken as a perfect example of the changing fashions of their eras. Adlestrop Park started its life as a humble barn south-east of the church which was then converted into a house. A long panelled room with a wooden fireplace and a staircase have been retained from this building. A classical porch on the frontage and gateposts bearing the Leigh crest of unicorn heads were added in about 1700. William Leigh III had a formal garden made in the first half of the eighteenth century which was recalled by Mary Leigh:

> ...the Gardens (in the old fashion) were remarkably pretty — ornamented with a canal, Fountain & several alcoves & expensive shewy summerhouses, one decorated with historic painting. In my remembrance there was an Orangerie; & when the Bowling Green was destroyed (by modernizing the Gardens) it might be said that one of the best accustomed Greens in England was no more for there seldom was a fine day in which yr hospitable Grandfather surrounded by his neighbours did not use it.[19]

The garden was also famous for its roses but between 1759 and 1763, after his father's death in 1757, James Leigh not only changed his house but this lovely garden too – blowing away the old formal style favoured by his forebears for a new Rococo pleasure ground laid out by Samuel Driver. Samuel Driver is usually described as 'nurseryman' but by training he was a surveyor. Driver was also a garden advisor to Sir Edward Turner[20], James' brother-in-law. The paths were winding and the flowerbeds and shrubberies curved and new varieties of plants were planted as well as tried and true favourites. The plan for the garden features a mound with a garden temple or summerhouse to be reached through clumps of trees – nothing of this remains and whether it was actually built out we do not know. A Chinese bridge and a winding canal, cascade and irregular pool all featured in quite a small area.[21]

James Leigh restocked the gardens as can be seen in a bill

sent to him in 1752 for new trees, flowers and vegetables for the kitchen garden. There is an evocative list of flowers ranging from 'Hollyhocks, Loves lies Bleeding, Blue lupins and Stript Columbines' which could come out of any modern-day nursery catalogue. There were also over twenty varieties of roses and distinctive shrubs and trees such as 'Maple Leav'd Tulip Tree', 'Carolina Cluster Cherry' a 'perfum'd Cherry' and the Handerchief Tree, Catalpa.[22] Ten years later more trees were planted including a Cedar of Lebanon which cost eight shillings plus a hundred common flowering shrubs (cost: one pound five shillings) and, for the table, a huge quantity of 600 asparagus plants (cost nine shillings). In 1765 there is an agreement with a gardener for the upkeep of the Pleasure Grounds, the garden, plantations, gravel, shrubbery, upkeep of the trees, the Summer House and the kitchen garden ensuring a regular supply of everything from salad greens to melons and cucumbers. The contract states that William Bricknell was to be paid 'Thirty-eight pounds a year' including his 'Diet & Lodging.'[23] In present days terms this would be a modest annual wage of about seven and a half thousand pounds.

> 'The number of acres contained in this garden was such as Catherine could not listen to without dismay... the walls seemed countless in number, endless in length; a village of hot-houses seemed to arise among them, and a whole parish to be at work among them.' *Northanger Abbey*

Meanwhile much of the old house was torn down and rebuilt and enlarged. The first works at Adlestrop Park were to build a two-storey block with a bay window on the south side of the house and in 1759-63 this was enlarged to take its present form. A local mason from Stow on the Wold, William Hitchcox, undertook the work on the original extension for £300.[24] Hitchcox was the architect's preferred builder but just like some modern builders he was slow to complete this work and so the later building was entrusted to Thomas and Samuel Collett – another local business – who were felt to be more reliable.

The architect for the new house was Sanderson Miller who 'designed the exquisite southwest front in his imaginative style of Gothick.'[25] Beautifully stylised with crocketed pinnacles and decorated stonework it is symmetrical with a central gable flanked on each side by smaller ones. The buttresses on the corners are crowned in an echo of medieval chimneys. Large mullioned windows face the parkland and the whole has a sense of delicacy and lightness; it is this side that is always shown in early prints and photographs. It was an imaginative and innovative choice of style by James Leigh and quite different from the standard Georgian pile of Godmersham House or the Jacobean grandeur of Chastleton. It drew attention to the village as the historian Samuel Rudd in his *New History of Gloucestershire*, first published in 1779, noted: 'He (James Leigh) hath greatly repaired and enlarged the old family seat, in the Gothick taste and resides there.' The friendship between the Leighs and their chosen architect, Sanderson Miller, went back to 1750 when they met at a neighbour's dinner party on 3 May where the notion of applying his skills to Adlestrop House must have been part of the conversation. Soon after this occasion, Miller went to Adlestrop Park 'measuring etc. for the new room' returning on 22 August, walking 'with Mr J.Leigh to the stone pit near Chastleton, making estimate of new Rom'.[26]

Sanderson Miller was famed for his Gothic follies notably the faux castle tower built at Wimpole Hall in Cambridgeshire and his restyling of his own Elizabethan house, Radway Grange in Warwickshire in the Gothic style. At Radway he added a thatched cottage *ornée* and an octagonal tower in his grounds. He was arguably a pioneer in applying this style in England – earlier than Horace Walpole at Strawberry Hill or Robert Mylne at Blaise Castle, for instance. At a later period a large square dovecote with four gables was also erected some way apart from the main house to the north-east.

This was the elegant house with its Rococo garden and profuse planting and gently curved paths that Jane Austen saw on her first visits to the village in 1794 and 1796 and doubtless enjoyed, admiring the colourful flower borders and walking the short distance to the wooded mound. But all this was to change before she returned to the village in 1806. The years in between her visits were tumultuous ones for Jane. An abortive flirtation with Tom Lefroy came to nothing, Cassandra experienced the death of her fiancé, Tom Fowle in 1797 and, perhaps most upsetting of all, in December 1800 Jane was told, without any warning, that her parents were leaving her childhood home in Steventon and she must accompany them to Bath. Sad times affected her cousins in Adlestrop too – in 1797 the rector's wife, Mary, died at the age of sixty-five. This seems to have sparked off a new urge in the vicar to make drastic improvements both to the parsonage grounds and to those of his nephew at Adlestrop Park – detailed in the following chapter. Perhaps it was a way to distract himself from his grief. The couple, having married late in life, had never had a family and although his sister, Elizabeth was at the rectory and presumably took over the running of the household, the loss of his witty and erudite companion left a considerable gap in his life.

One thing that hardly changed was the church of St Mary Magdalene in Adlestrop, home of all the Adlestrop Leigh memorials and burials as well as villagers' graves over the last four hundred years. Originally the church was a chapelry of Broadwell in the Stow Deanery and so the rector officiated at both villages, although in 1535 there was a chaplain at Adlestrop who received £5.6s.8d. from the rector of Broadwell. The rector seems to have moved to Adlestrop in 1540 where he built himself a house. Because of its early connection to Broadwell Adlestrop's dead were buried there before 1580, although there is some evidence of interments within the village from 1516 and of baptisms and weddings from 1538.[27] A certain confusion over which parish had the rector and which was a chaplaincy or curacy continued for some years in church records but in reality after the seventeenth century it was Adlestrop that housed the rector and the Leighs who owned the living. The church is not of any architectural significance but its quiet presence, the glimpses of its weathered grey tower on the approaches to the village and the sound of the clock chiming the hour all play their part in the tranquil and timeless atmosphere. The crenellated tower is fourteenth century and the chancel arch thirteenth century but the church has been restored several times – twice within the eighteenth century because of the poor quality of the labourers as Mary Leigh reported:

> The body of Adlestrop Church has been built twice within these thirty years, owing to the carelessness or roguery of the builder…the principal part of the expense your Father took upon himself…[28]

This refers to work done in 1750 and again in 1765 – the later work probably undertaken by Sanderson Miller. The chancel was altered in 1824 and the whole church restored in the 1860s – even the windows were remodelled – so it is not surprising that little of its medieval past remains apart from the fifteenth-century font. Outside the south wall are Leigh family tombs enclosed by a railing and the whole interior has monuments and memorials to the family on the floors and walls. There are diamond-shaped hatchments of the family on the upper walls of the nave showing the intermarriages with the Twisletons – James Henry's marriage to Julia and an earlier one celebrating the connection with the Brydges family when James married into the ducal Chandos clan. The hatchments' paint and significance would have been fresh and new to Jane Austen's eyes and she must have read and pondered on the many Leigh memorials while she listened to her cousin's sermons.

When the family vault under the south transept was first created in 1774 a macabre sight met the eyes of the workmen: '...very deep were found sixteen human skeletons, thrown promiscuously over each other; perhaps thus buried after some Battle'.[29]

The Revd Thomas Leigh was also intrigued by parish history and made notes about it and the burials in the churchyard.

The Adlestrop registers date back to 1538 and the some of the oldest names found in them are: Fretherne, Newman, Grenehill, Wylobe or Willoughby, Collabor, Freman, Mydminter, Price, Dadley and Tidmarsh.

He mentions some of the oldest gravestones and memorials in the church and churchyard such as the stone tablet on the outside north wall of the chancel embellished with a skull which commemorates Anthony Greenhill who died in 1596 and his wife, Anne. It was erected by his son-in-law, Thomas Dadlee. Even two centuries ago the Reverend Thomas Leigh could not read the inscriptions on:

the heavy Altar tomb ...very handsomely carved with two cherubs supporting a central shield, the panels of the stone representing grapes and other devices — the inscription on this tomb is so faint that it is impossible to make out to whom it was erected.

This can still be seen in the churchyard among other gravestones half sunk in the ground with their inscriptions totally eroded with moss and lichen. He notes the several stones erected behind the chancel to the Tidmarsh family and:

A quaint Epitaph runs thus: 'H.I. Joseph the youngest son of Richard Hanks of this place, a youth of pregnant parts, great hopes and innate probity, snacht away from his

Friends (who were All who knew him) by a Quinsey, June the 18th, 1719, aged 14 years & 5 months....The epitaphs on the stones erected to John Shaylor and his wife are of interest because of the Shaylor Charity (gift of bread) by which the poor still benefit.

These gravestones adjoin the south transept in the churchyard and the words can just be made out with the help of shafts of sunlight upon them:

Here lies the body of John Shaylor
who died May 26, 1803, aged 77 years

The while he was alive on earth
He was a neighbour good,
He often did relieve the poor
With money food and wood,
And now he's laid within the grave
He have left a trifle still
To be yearly given to the poor
It was his own good will

This was the same John Shaylor, one of eight farmers, who in 1763 made an agreement with Revd Leigh for a four-year lease of lands for which he paid a rent of ten pounds and three shillings plus a tithe great and small. He obviously was wealthy enough to pay the rent and to leave a small charitable legacy but was no doubt regarded as a social inferior by the Leighs.

The clock and the fine arch and lantern over the gateway into the churchyard would not have been seen by the Austens as the clock was installed to celebrate the Golden Jubilee of Queen Victoria and the arch her Diamond Jubilee.

CHAPTER FIVE

Country Society in a Century of Change

'I am conscious of being far better reconciled to a country residence that I had ever expected to be.... An elegant, moderate-sized house in the centre of family connections — continual engagements among them — commanding the first society in the neighbourhood...' **Mary Crawford to Fanny Price,** *Mansfield Park*

Jane Austen's characters are often ambivalent about country life. To some, like the eponymous Emma, life at Highbury with its quiet routines is all she has ever known and for her there is sufficient stimulus in her environment to satisfy her. For others like Mary Crawford or Lady Susan – complex and sophisticated town ladies – the countryside seems a dreary and dull place. Country living was the norm in Jane Austen's time when four-fifths of England's nine million people lived in villages or hamlets and the remaining fifth in small towns – London was the only city of huge size.

'I take London in my way to that insupportable spot, a country village, for I am really going to Churchhill' *Letter from Lady Susan to Mrs Johnson: Lady Susan*

How would Jane have looked on Adlestrop and Gloucestershire? Even the Leighs, who were very fond of the village, saw it as old-fashioned yet felt a profound attachment towards it as this anecdote recounted by Mary Leigh in her Family History reveals:

... James Leigh the 2nd son of the first Theo Leigh who died aged 21 in June 1713. He returned to Adlestrop in deep consumption. He was attended by a great Oxford doctor who came to Adlestrop to attend him: the Coach was at the door to carry him to an airing, the honest doctor hinted to the old gentleman (young man's father) that it was a forlorn hope "You are (replied Theophilus) Doctor a young and timorous practitioner: nor do you know what a Panacea Adlestrop hill air is to all the Leighs?" Yet — not withstanding its salubrity, the boy died the next day.[1]

Apart from this strong attachment to place one of the most important considerations to the middle and upper classes was how many other similar families there were in their neighbourhood for socialising with. Adlestrop certainly had a good circle of substantial houses within the immediate vicinity – Chastleton House, Banks Fee at Longborough, Broadwell Manor, Sezincote, Bourton House, Upper Swell Manor, Oddington House, Swerford Park, Maugersbury Manor, Daylesford House and a little further afield Farnborough House, Radway, Broughton Castle and, of course, the other Leighs at Stoneleigh Abbey in Warwickshire. In the whole of Gloucestershire over 440 improvements and new buildings of country houses are recorded in the period between 1660 and 1830 which gives us some idea of the density of families with a substantial income.

The neighbourhood certainly met Mrs Bennet's boast of dining with four and twenty families but despite this society the Leighs at Adlestrop Park and Stoneleigh spent a lot of their time in London, Bath or nearby Cheltenham. It was probably essential to do so to consult their bankers, brokers and lawyers in person and to partake of sophisticated amusements during the Season. In later life Jane Austen herself thoroughly enjoyed her trips to London when she stayed with her brother Henry.

She was able to go to the art galleries in London where she amused hearself by finding portrait matches to her own characters in her books:

> Henry and I went to the Exhibition in Spring Gardens. It is not thought a good collection, but I was very well pleased—particularly...with a small portrait of Mrs Bingley, excessively like her. I went in hope of seeing one of her Sister, but there was no Mrs Darcy.[2]

With her brother and other friends Jane attended the theatre, seeing famous actors such as Edmund Kean as Shylock at Drury Lane and other lighter entertainments in the form of musicals. She told Cassandra of her delight in bowling along the grand streets and parks in an open barouche – 'I liked my solitary elegance very much, & was ready to laugh all the time, at my being where I was'.[3]

This was certainly Jane Austen's version of living the high life in contrast to the pitfalls of living in the countryside, especially in the winter months. In London we can see Jane as a keen tourist, enjoying the novelties and diversions, but never feeling herself capable of becoming part of city life. Yet her novels frankly often acknowledge the dull tedium that could attend country living. In an unusual moment of depression Emma reflects on being without her companion Miss Taylor and sixteen miles away from her sister and alone with her valetudinarian father: '...many a long October and November evening must be struggled through'.[4]

'But I, who live in a small retired village in the country, can never find greater sameness in such a place like this [Bath] than in my own home; for here are a variety of amusements, a variety of things to be seen and done all day long, which I can know nothing of there...one day in the country is exactly like another'. *Catherine Morland, Northanger Abbey*

Indubitably the world of the small town or country village was the one Jane Austen knew best and the one she returned to in all her works. The structure and economic viability of that world is the solid backdrop to her imaginary players. The life of the agricultural labourer or small farmer, or tradesman seems absent from the brilliant carapace of the action – only intruding occasionally. But she was very attentive to what was happening to the countryside and how rapidly it was changing thanks to two main developments in the eighteenth century – the acts of enclosure and the craze for 'improvements' to a gentleman's estate. This chapter describes how the acts of enclosure affected the grassroots of the community while favouring the landed gentry and clergy in Adlestrop.

The Cotswolds, especially the northern part where Adlestrop is placed, did not benefit or even participate in the beginnings of the Industrial Revolution but remained a stubbornly agricultural region, apart from stone and slate quarrying. There were small-scale enterprises such as the silk mills in Blockley and Chipping Campden as early as 1700 where a cheap labour force and a good supply of fast running streams in the village aided the operation. The water supply was also ideal for paper manufacture for a century and a half, between 1750 and 1900 in places such as Stanway and Barrington. Areas near Stroud in south Gloucestershire were much more go-ahead and a whole weaving industry sprang up in the steep narrow valleys to accommodate the needs of a growing population.

'Hence we came to the famous Cotswold-Downs, so eminent for the best of sheep, and finest wools in England...'
A Tour Through the Whole Island of Great Britain,
Daniel Defoe

Medieval prosperity and the building of the market towns and larger churches in places such as Chipping Campden, Winchcombe and Northleach were due to the flourishing of the wool trade and hardy Cotswold sheep. As early as the fourteenth century the wool from the region was famous with Italian merchants who sent their emissaries to Northleach (*Norlecchio*), Burford (*Boriforte*) and Cirencester (*Sirisesti*) to buy up stocks. The best and most costly Italian fabrics were woven from English wool.[5] The Cotswolds were known to them as *in Chondisgualdo* – a guide book *La pratica della Mercatura*, dated *c*.1315, included a list of the main producers. These were the monastic houses such as Evesham Abbey with its estates in the Cotswolds which originally included Adlestrop. The numbers of the flocks were large. Evesham produced 10 sacks – the equivalent to 1500 sheep while Winchcombe outdid this with 40 sacks representing 6000 sheep. The wool was listed at 11 marks per sack and each sack contained about 150 fleeces. At Chipping Campden Roger de Somery grazed 1000 sheep on the common pasture of 'the Wold' but the ordinary village farmer probably had a good deal fewer than 100 sheep. Before widespread enclosures, ordinary cottagers kept a few sheep and sold their wool – one of the few ways they had to augment their low wages.[6] In the summer the flocks were put on hill pastures and moved down to the valleys in the winter where they were fed on peas, beans and hay.[7] These were common crops in Adlestrop throughout the centuries.

It is likely that Adlestrop farmers would have taken their sheep to the nearest town, Stow on the Wold, which had a market charter from 1107 and was renowned for its trade up to Georgian times. Daniel Defoe recorded that up to 20,000 sheep were sold in a single day there. The town is constructed with a host of narrow alley ways knows as 'tures' leading to the market square to facilitate driving sheep down to the market pens and it is no surprise that its main street goes by the name of 'Sheep Street'. Yet the smallness of Adlestrop church compared to others in the area does not lead one to conclude that great riches came to the village during the golden years of the wool trade. Over the centuries demand for Cotswold wool fell – some believed that the wool became inferior through

'He had a very fine flock... he had been bid more for his wool than any body in the country.' *Emma*

the interbreeding of stock. Finer wool was sought from Spain and Germany by fashionable clothiers while Cotswold wool was used for heavy cloth. George III tried to help falling trade when he imported a flock of merino sheep from Spain via the help of Sir Joseph Banks of the Royal Society, who noted in 1802, 'the demand for his Majesty's merino sheep had increased prodigiously, especially in Gloucestershire'.[8] But slowly with enclosure the wolds were turned into arable fields with stone walls and sheep were no longer the leading factor in the Cotswold agricultural economy.

Adlestrop was never a prosperous community and even its leading family as we have seen, had to retrench in the early part of the eighteenth century when William Leigh undertook exile in Utrecht for five years to avoid the outgoings of English gentry life. Throughout England the aims of the aristocracy and the gentry were to enlarge their estates as the more land one owned, the more money and influence would follow. Dynastic marriages also strengthened families and added to their holdings. There was much rebuilding and improving of mansions and grounds. The dukes and money men who owned the great houses such as Blenheim Palace, Castle Howard, Studley Royal, Stourhead and Woburn Abbey spent money like water on new buildings and landscaping their land. They were keen to advertise their wealth and their examples were followed throughout society. In Adlestrop the Leighs' fortunes improved sufficiently over the eighteenth century to join in with these extravagances.

The wars with France and the blockade around England's shores put an end to the Grand Tour so beloved of young aristocrats. Society turned inwards, appreciating the beauties of the British landscape and spending money there rather than abroad. Landowners began to improve the fertility of their land and agricultural innovations included the introduction of the turnip in the 1730s; the four-fold rotation of crops championed by Lord Townshend whereby wheat, turnips, barley and clover were grown for fodder and grazing to ensure year-round breeding of livestock; and Jethro Tull's development in seed drilling and hoeing. In Adlestrop the leases made with tenant farmers included strict covenants on which crops they should grow, which lands should lie fallow and how they should be rotated year by year over the period of the tenancy.

At first the majority ignored these novel schemes and the age-old open-field strip system where crops and stock were controlled and shared by the whole community continued – this was a system whereby the poor could grow more food and graze a family cow or a small number of sheep to add to their meagre wages as farm labourers. Each villager would be allotted strips of arable land from the open field together with a share of hay and space for their animals. This was a 'yardland' or 'virgate' from the Latin *virga* which means 'rod'. A traditional ceremony of giving land to a new holder was symbolised by handing a rod to him. This still occurred as late as 1694 in Burford and later still in 1744 in Guiting Power so it doubtless also occurred in Adlestrop.[9] A carefully drawn diagram in the mid-eighteenth century of an Adlestrop field called Fulwell to the 'Scale of ½ a Inch to a Chain' illustrates the complexity of the strip system in operation.[10] As well as an allowance for Glebe i.e. land owned by the church, the field is divided between no less than ten people including several members of the Leigh family, tenant farmers and villagers. There are thirty-two strips in all, some larger than others, but the arrangement shows that the owners' strips were dotted all over the field thereby making productive use of them doubly difficult.

It is interesting to take a brief look at the numbers of people who would have taken advantage of this system in the village and the figures show that up to 1650 the village population was fairly static and the shared strips yielded enough for their needs. In the Domesday survey of 1086 the entry is brief:

> The church itself holds Adlestrop. There are 7 hides. In desmene are 2 ploughs; and 10 villans and 2 bordars with 3 ploughs. There are 4 slaves, and 1 knight with 2 ploughs. There is little meadow. It was worth 4l now 100s.

The church was St Mary of Evesham. A hide was an approximate area of land calculated for assessing tax liabilities possibly about 120 acres which would be divided into four yardlands or virgates. The term 'plough' implied a team of up to eight oxen and the plough itself – so in the 'desmene', the land in the personal possession of the landholder, there were two ploughs and the knight had the same. The ten villans or villeins, were freemen and of higher status than the peasant bordars and between them there were three ploughs – implying that they also had land to till. The slaves belonged to the knight and were the lowest in the social strata. Further records show a male population of 21 in 1327. In Elizabethan times 18 households were recorded in 1563; 19 in 1650. In 1608, John Smith compiled a record of the able-bodied men in Gloucestershire who were capable of bearing arms. This gives a little more detail about those living in Adlestrop at that time.[11]

William Leigh (I) is listed as the lord of the village, there are thirteen husbandmen, seven labourers, only one artisan – a mason by trade, and nine servants. So now Domesday's ten villeins have turned into thirteen free tenant farmers described as husbandmen, and the number of labourers has increased to seven. Only Thomas Fretherne is listed as the owner of a 'Corslet fur' (a light musket) and only seven men are described as trained soldiers. Thomas Fretherne is wealthy enough to have three servants and Margaret Fretherne, a widow – perhaps his mother – has two. The village is charged with finding 'two Corslets and one Calyver' for the local militia.

In Stow on the Wold there are many more occupations given among the townsfolk: one innkeeper, four butchers, two masons, one baker, an ironmonger, a glover, a cobbler and five shoemakers, two cheesemongers, a tinker, three 'slatters' (probably meaning roof tilers), two tailors, a mercer plus one weaver of fustian and two ordinary weavers and a fuller – the last all engaged in the cloth or wool trade. Compared to Adlestrop there was considerable diversity of livelihoods and more opportunities besides eking out a living from the land. The village husbandmen would have had leases of land from William Leigh as well as a share of the common land. The open field system was inefficient farming for subsistence rather than profit. Efficient arable farming became more of a necessity and was encouraged by government. More land was needed and to acquire it the existing landowners, including the clergy, enclosed the open fields as they had the capital to employ solicitors and lawyers to draw up the documents allowing them to do so. The landowners also controlled the two Houses of Parliament which passed the acts. This table shows how the land grab grew in Jane Austen's lifetime:

Number of enclosure acts per decade

1750-60	156
1760-70	424
1770-80	642
1780-90	287
1790-1800	506
1800-1810	906[12]

In Gloucestershire incumbents received 12,000 acres and laymen around 8,000.

The old common land became incorporated into new and existing farms and a host of new walls and hedges were built to show their demarcation, making the attractive picture of small parcels of land we see in the Cotswold landscape today which Jane Austen would also have enjoyed. After enclosure the land use was often altered so the old downs were put to the plough and arable strips returned to grass for larger flocks of animals to graze on.

James Leigh loved to record his thoughts and musings in writing. He faithfully set down records of all his accounts, leaseholdings in the village and other property he owned in England in 1761 besides Adlestrop.[13] This included rents and leases in the nearby villages of Longborough and Shipston and further afield in Kent and most oddly a 99-year lease which paid him a ground rent of £40 per annum at the notorious Marshalsea Prison in south London which he noted was 'part of my unsettled estate.' He was also seriously thinking about the pros and cons of enclosure:

There is I think no Reason to doubt, if all the 32 yard Lands in Adlestrop Field were fallen into my Hands & that I had money sufficient to spare from other purposes or full power to charge the Estate with the whole sum requisite for this purpose, but that even upon the principles I have hitherto gone an Inclosure might be safely & advantageously undertaken at Adlestrop... the Improvement would pay very good Interest for the whole sum laid out (Buildings &c all included) & likewise Yield some clear Gain to the Proprietor besides the Satisfaction he would enjoy in the Thoughts of having his estate put in the best Condition possible & every thing about him right & convenient.

Surely the most telling phrase here is his desire to leave his estate in the best condition possible. This idea of good husbandry and taking care of your own property for the benefit of your heirs is exactly what a Mr Knightley or even a Mr Darcy would undertake to the approval of their creator.

Unfortunately James Leigh did not survive to see his wishes

realised as his sudden death just preceded the 1775 enclosure act for 'Dividing and Inclosing the Common Fields, and other Commonable Lands and Grounds within the manor of Adlestrop in the County of Glocester'.[14] The beneficiaries of the Act were his son, still a minor, James Henry Leigh, his brother and his wife. The reason given for the enclosure was 'the said Fields lying intermixed and dispersed, and being in their present State in a great Measure incapable of Improvement...' This was the crux of the matter and the Act allowed the Leighs a free hand in pulling down cottages, carrying off the materials they were built with, enclosing whatever they wished, putting up new fences, making new roads and paths and erecting new buildings as convenient to them.

The legal expenses were considerable as a lawyer's bill of 2 November 1776 shows.[15] The total price of £274.14.5 covered everything from printing the bill, hearing it read, soliciting the act and attendance on Lady Caroline. I suspect some of this money came from Elizabeth Wentworth although the Revd. Thomas had to seek permission 'under strict conditions and open accounting' from the Bishop of Gloucester to borrow £400 to pay for fencing and building on the lands allotted to him. James Leigh could rest easily in his grave secure that his wished-for improvement of his estate had been completed and legally approved.

Enclosure did not benefit the local tradesmen or other families in Adlestrop – they were now landless and could not catch rabbits, graze animals, allow pigs to forage, or collect gleanings, berries and wood for fuel. They only had their cottage gardens to grow vegetables in and pick fruit from a few apple or pear trees if they were lucky. On a national scale these people would leave their country homes and drift to towns where employment could be found in the first stirrings of the Industrial Revolution. Mechanisation meant fewer people were necessary to help with the harvest and women and children who had worked alongside their menfolk gradually became unwanted in the fields. The amount spent on Poor Relief in the village rose sharply between 1775 and 1803, much more so than in neighbouring villages. A document in the Gloucester Archives shows a note in the Revd. Thomas Leigh's own hand listing the Poor Rates from 1772 to 1801 recording a huge leap in payments over the decade.

1791	£74
1792	£87
1793	£104
1794	£71
1795	£87
1796	£122
1797	£153
1798	£114
1799	£246
1800	£243
1801	£342[16]

The population of the village had risen from 1700 onwards and of the forty-one families in 1803 almost half were in receipt of regular relief funding. This was partly due to the high price of grain during the French Wars and subsequent blockade which meant than corn could not be imported from Europe which, in turn, increased bread prices. There had been a series of poor harvests and in the spring of 1795 a spate of riots over food prices. These factors coupled with the increase in village numbers and very low wages in the countryside meant privation for many. In Adlestrop labourers were paid as little as 10d a day by Samuel Driver in the work on the gardens at Adlestrop Park in 1752.

'…in observing the appearance of the country, the bearings of the roads, the difference of soil, the state of the harvest, the cottages, the cattle, the children, she found entertainment…' *Fanny Price on the drive to Sotherton, Mansfield Park*

Children were paid 4d a day and Driver earned 5 shillings a day[17] (a lot less than Repton). Just over twenty years later Lady Caroline's account book prepared for her by William Beman shows that the labourers 'Thomas Newman, Joseph Newman, John Kempson, John Keen, Thomas Eden paid for 6 days work 6 shillings.'[18] So an average wage for a day's work for an unskilled man was a mere shilling. As Park Honan observes in his biography what Jane Austen would later see when she lived in Chawton she had already been exposed to in Gloucestershire some years before:

> All of its land had been enclosed in the eighteenth century. Wealthier landowners felt that this, of course was truly progress! Families at the lower fringes of the yeomanry, though, suffered cruelly when they lost the right to graze a cow or a few sheep on common land. The medieval common lands had all been fenced in. Poor farmers gradually had been pushed down into the ranks of wage labourers; ironically they would have to buy their food, instead of raise it, and at prices that climbed steadily until 1813. In *Mansfield Park* and *Emma* a deep feeling about land and the community is a response to what Jane Austen saw and heard in her Chawton years. [19]

The rising levels of the poor was a national problem: local magistrates in the Berkshire village of Speen near Newbury met in the Pelican Inn on 6 May, 1795 worried about the level of relief stating: 'the present state of the poor law requires further assistance than has generally been given them.' They thought it would be fair to bring in a scale of allowances depending on the recipient's family circumstances – an early form of what we see now in our welfare state with family tax credits and child benefits. For every penny more than a shilling that a loaf cost, each man would have three pence more for himself and a penny more for each member of his family. The magistrates also suggested that landowners and farmers should pay better wages but this idea fell on stony ground. It was also assumed that those who were better off would do their duty to the poor and Jane's characters, like her own family, often engage in charitable visits. In one of her letters she mentions this task:

> We are just beginning to be engaged in another Christmas Duty, & next to eating Turkies, a very pleasant one, laying out Edward's money for the Poor; & the sum that passes through our hands this year is considerable, as Mrs Knight left £20 to the Parish.[20]

Social divisions were rigid as Emma reminded Harriet Smith who wanted to accept the marriage proposal from gentleman-farmer, Robert Martin: '…it would have been the loss of a friend to me. I could not have visited Mrs Robert Martin of Abbey-Mill Farm.' Of course Emma is castigated by the fair and sensible Mr Knightley over her snobbery and in the end she does condescend to accept 'knowing' Mr and Mrs Robert Martin. Her difficulty with the Martins shows how strong class distinctions were despite them being a respectable family who had lived and worked their farm for generations and were prosperous enough to employ labourers and servants of their own. Robert Martin is also keen on farming improvements and 'reads the Agricultural Reports'.

'Emma was very compassionate; and the distresses of the poor were as sure of relief from her personal attention and kindness, her counsel and patience, as from her purse. She understood their ways, could allow for their ignorance and their temptations, had no romantic expectations of extraordinary virtues from those, for whom education had done so little.' *Emma*

The Leighs consolidation of their ownership of land was symptomatic of national change. First they had altered their leaseholds to be held in the lessor's lifetime rather than on the older 'copyhold' principle which could be handed on from tenant to tenant. James Leigh halved the numbers of farmers holding land from eight in 1763 to four in 1767 and then down to just two in 1774. Immediately after James' death the inventory made at that time lists recently enclosed lands near the Great House as: 'ancient meadows – Fulwells, a new Inclosed Close, Gavon, Norton Gap Ground, Crabtree Furlong'.[21] Also noted is 'The piece of ground lately taken in called The Pleasure Ground never to be stocked but with sheep only'. The land enclosed after the 1775 harvest by way of the Adlestrop Inclosure Act allotted about 125 acres to the rector in respect of his glebe and tithes. The sole Copyholder was assigned 22 acres and the Lord of the Manor 553 acres which formed three farms of 250, 258 and 45 acres. Adlestrop Hill, referred to as Green Hill made up the remaining 226 acres and was not enclosed but still belonged to the Leighs.[22]

In *A Thousand Years of the English Parish*, the historian Dr Anthea Jones notes:

> Where this [enclosure] occurred, it made a big alteration to their [the clergy's] relationship with their parishioners; they ceased to be tax-collectors and became landowners.... enclosure involved large-scale reorganisation of the fields and could not proceed without the agreement of the tithe owner. In the open field system cultivators shared the local resources of the land, cooperating in their style of husbandry to the general good.

Following the 1775 enclosure farmhouses were built including Hillside Farm (known as Parsonage Farm until 1947) and let with common and fuel rights on Adlestrop Hill. Fern Farm, built some ten years earlier, has a barn beside it and about

600 yards beyond the farmhouse lies the ruins of Hill Barn. Near to this is a field where an ancient oak stands, now used mainly for grazing cattle, where the old landscape of ridge and furrow and strip farming system can clearly be seen. Its undulating ground has never been ploughed. In 1801 the village's arable acreage was 316 acres and the main crops of wheat, barley, peas and beans remained the same as those found in the fields in 1498. Only small amounts of oats and turnips were grown. In 1801 the rector lists an 'Accounts of the different kinds of Corn. The Produce of the Harvest 1801'

'...the gentlemen had supplied the discourse with some variety—the variety of politics, inclosing land, and breaking horses...'
Sense and Sensibility

Wheat: £106
Barley: £96
Beans and Pease: £55
Oats: £31
Potatoes: (unclear)
Turnips: £20

The numbers of sheep were declining and they, along with cattle were pastured in the valley. Today the meadow beyond Adlestrop Park (the old Pleasure Ground) provides grazing for a huge flock of sheep with their young lambs in the late spring and early summer.

The estimate for the building of Fern Farm still exists in the records written in a flourishing copperplate hand dated 21 December 1766.[23] Its heading is 'An Estimate for a New Farm House for Ja. Leigh Esq. at Adlestrop to be Built in Fern Grounds'. Everything is carefully worked out with all the details for the costs for the Masons, Carpenters, Plasterers, Glazeing and the hundreds of feet of timber, oak and elm for beams, floors and rafters. For instance: 'Paveing Kitching, Parlowar, Pantrey, Brewhouse & Dairey with Adlestrop Hill House 926 feet at 3d per foot including Caridge…£11.12 shillings.' A new oven and, 'Making What Draines Shall be Wanting and a Little Pitching at Doors' would cost 5 shillings. The total estimate plus the timber comes to just under £250. A very fair price to pay for a farmhouse that still overlooks the village, almost 250 years later.

In the nineteenth century Adlestrop had four working farms but gradually the traditional way of life in the village changed and much working activity ceased when mechanised machinery began to be used, such as milking machines and combine harvesters. The farms let many of their workmen go creating unemployment, about half the population moved away in search of work and one thing led to another. The number of tradesmen declined

'…he had to tell what every field was to bear next year…the plan of a drain, the change of a fence, the felling of a tree, and the destination of every acre for wheat, turnips or spring corn was entered into…'
A description of Mr Knightley, Emma

from eight in 1811 to just three in 1821. The shops closed as demand ebbed away and many of the delivery carts simply stopped coming down the hill from Stow on the Wold.

Now there is only one main farm where the current Lord Leigh lives and farms: Fern Farm. It is owned by the Adlestrop Settlement Trust which was set up in 1965 by Rupert Leigh, Lord Leigh's grandfather, to protect the family's land and property holdings in the village from being broken up and sold. Lord Leigh believes his grandfather wanted the family connection to Adlestrop to continue in perpetuity. The Leigh family are the sole beneficiaries of the Trust which today owns about 1,300 acres which includes some of the 1,051 acres enclosed in 1775.

Hillside Farm has long been a private house and is now facing demolition to be replaced by a modern mansion, designed by

Prince Charles' favoured architects, and lived in by the twenty-first century's version of a plutocrat – the investment banker. Its outbuildings will include modern 'pleasure grounds' of a tennis court, swimming pool and stables to take six hunters so the owner can participate in the Heythrop Hunt.

Fern Farm is a mixed farm with about 300 acres for arable crops of mainly wheat and rape, 150 acres is 'set aside' in environmentally friendly fields to encourage birdlife, butterflies and wild flowers. Woodland for timber accounts for another 300 acres. Lord Leigh has his own horses and a livery stable for about 20 or more horses at any given time. No one in the village now works on the farm. Outside contractors are brought in with giant harvesters for the crops and save for a sole gamekeeper and his dog who patrol the hills and coverts, the fields are usually deserted. The exception to this are the many ramblers who use the network of footpaths across the scenic valleys.

It is ironic that the only farmer in Adlestrop to remain is the landholder himself – Lord Leigh benefiting from over five hundred years of family ownership. This continuity would please Jane Austen although I am sure she would have been saddened at the loss of a vibrant traditional way of life. She was well aware of the economies of farming, the enclosures and the inequalities of the age-old hierarchical system but it was a part of life, as unchanging as the seasons and she would have had no wish to alter it.

CHAPTER SIX

'Call in Repton': The Picturesque Movement in Fact and Fiction

'...a lecture in the picturesque immediately followed, in which his instructions were so clear that she soon began to see beauty in everything admired by him...he talked of foregrounds, distances and second-distances; side-screens and perspectives ; lights and shades...' **Northanger Abbey**

Adlestrop was to provide Jane Austen with a first-hand experience of how following the Romantic or Picturesque Movement could result in profound change. Through staying at Adlestrop parsonage with her cousins she witnessed a drastic alteration to the village landscape and also found out about the most famous improver of the age, Humphry Repton. Repton was directly employed by the Revd Thomas Leigh and his nephew and it is certain that Repton and his work would have been a conversational topic over the mutton and rhubarb at the dinner table. Repton is one of the few real people to appear in her fiction by name and Jane Austen felt confident enough in her knowledge of his methods and his famous fees to draw him so closely into the plot of *Mansfield Park*. The subject of improvements to the landscape appears in all of her novels one way or another but in *Mansfield Park* it becomes a central motif and metaphor.

Jane Austen carefully checked all her own references, for instance in a letter to her favourite niece, Anna, commenting on Anna's own novel she pointed out possible factual blunders.

Jane had read it aloud to her mother and sister and her letter comments on the characters, the plot and a multitude of other details. She counsels Anna: 'Let the Portmans go to Ireland, but as you know nothing of the Manners there, you had better not go with them. You will be in danger of giving false representations.'[1]

To avoid giving 'false representations' herself Jane's powers of observation and attention to detail were acute. At an early age she was aware of the ideas and the controversies surrounding the differing attitudes in late Georgian and Regency England towards the natural world and the landscape. The battle was fought not just on the ground itself but in art and literature, its influence branching out to thoughts on the sublime, human sensibility, Romanticism with a capital 'R', and the fascination with the antique and the Gothic. Jane was strongly under the spell of the Revd William Gilpin who published a series of illustrated books in the 1780s about beautiful areas of Britain. The books contained his own aquatints and also advice to his readers on how to appreciate the essence and rugged qualities of natural landscapes. Henry Tilney and his sister are keen advocates of Gilpin and Catherine Morland sees them 'viewing the country with the eyes of people accustomed to drawing; and decided on its capability of being formed into pictures with all the eagerness of real taste'.

'if you cd discover whether Northamptonshire is a County of Hedgerows, I shd be glad again.'
Letter 79 from Jane Austen to Cassandra 29 January 1813

Another strand of this concept was the ideas of the French philosopher Rousseau who believed that natural instincts should go hand in hand with nature itself, which he maintained was only beautiful when untamed. The concepts of the 'noble savage' and the goodness of the untutored mind were in sharp contrast to Georgian society's rules of self-control and order.

The Austen household was actively engaged in all the

new ideas of their time both through their addiction to contemporary fiction and through the journal *The Loiterer* which James and Henry Austen edited and contributed to during their Oxford days. Jane would eagerly read the latest issues brought home to Steventon by her lively elder brothers, which inspired her own first attempts at writing short pieces satirising the fads of the day. *The Loiterer*, like many student publications, was quite uncompromising and fulminated at:

> excess of sentiment and susceptibility which the works of the great Rouseau chiefly introduced, which ever subsequent Novel has since foster'd and which the voluptuous manners of the present age but too eagerly embrace.[2]

They had on their doorstep a prime example of the excesses and absurdities of the improvers in Rousseau's patron, Lord Harcourt, whose seat was at Nuneham Courtney, a village close to Oxford. Nearby was his ancestral home at Stanton-Harcourt but its setting meant that its views and prospects did not lend themselves to improvement. Lord Harcourt's solution to this problem was to choose the village of Nuneham Courtney itself for the siting of his new Palladian villa and grounds erasing the cottages from the scene in 1761 and rehousing his peasant tenants in a model village on the turnpike road.[3] In his defence Lord Harcourt saw the farm-workers' cottages as nothing more than 'tumble-down clay-built structures' – and they probably were overcrowded and in poor repair. In their place he had semi-detached cottages built with two rooms both downstairs and upstairs which were far more comfortable than the old hovels.

Bishop Porteus made a diary entry on 2 August 1800:

> Paid a visit to... Lord Harcourt at Nuneham. The village was originally in the Park at no great distance from the House and consisted of pretty white cottages, scattered

round a small piece of water and shaded by a number of very fine trees. The Late Lord Harcourt thinking the village too near the house, built the new one on the Oxford road...'[4]

This was an act which inspired Oliver Goldsmith's poem *The Deserted Village* which idealised the life of a country community:

> Sweet Auburn, loveliest village of the plain,
> Where health and plenty cheered the labouring swain,
>
> ...
>
> How often have I loitered o'er thy green,
> Where humble happiness endeared each scene;
> How often have I paused on every charm,
> The sheltered cot, the cultivated farm,
> The never-failing brook, the busy mill,
> The decent church that topped the neighbouring hill

Lord Harcourt pulled down the church 'that topped the neighbouring hill' and replaced it with an Athenian style temple, even levelling the churchyard, much to the distress of the parishioners. He wanted a garden that had no order or symmetry but looked like a wild forest glade. The Harcourts also followed Rousseau in encouraging good behaviour in the lower classes and were famous for handing out red letter 'M's for Merit for villagers who were industrious and kept their cottages clean. Jane's keen sense of humour could not resist making the Harcourts the subject of one of her pieces of adolescent juvenilia '*Henry and Eliza*'. She mocked the couple in the opening lines of her mini-novel:

> As Sir George and Lady Harcourt were superintending the Labour of their Haymakers, rewarding the industry of some by smiles of approbation, and punishing the idleness of others, by a cudgel...

Her interest in the subject continued throughout her life and one can see the trajectory of the cross-currents of the aesthetic concepts of the Georgian age in the behaviour of Jane Austen's heroines – from Marianne Dashwood's intense emotional responses in *Sense and Sensibility*, to Catherine Morland whose imagination runs wild in *Northanger Abbey* after immersing herself in Gothic horror novels. Elizabeth Bennett in *Pride and Prejudice* is more like her creator – enjoying quiet walks in the countryside and 'enamoured' of William Gilpin and his take on the Picturesque. In contrast quiet Fanny Price in *Mansfield Park* admires nature poetry and Cowper's work and expresses disquiet about the wholesale changes made by fitting in with the day's fashions. Emma wholeheartedly approves of established country values and Knightley's example of responsibility to the community; where changes were organic, they are normally praised but drastic alterations are presented as a threat to stability. Jane Austen's favourite poet, Cowper, in *The Task*, 'castigates "improvements" as "the idol of the age"'.[5]

Dorothy Wordsworth, the sister of the poet and a contemporary of Jane Austen, held a similar opinion. On a visit to Crowcombe Court in Somerset she recorded in her journal:

> Walked about the squire's grounds. Quaint waterfalls about, where Nature was very successfully striving to make beautiful what art had deformed—ruins, hermitages, &c., &c. In spite of all these things, the dell romantic and beautiful, though everywhere planted with unnaturalised trees. Happily we cannot shape the huge hill or carve out the valleys according to our fancy.[6]

Minor gentry such as the Leighs did not have the resources of the great aristocrats, but they too embarked on the Picturesque journey – James Leigh adopting the fashion for Gothic in his choice of architect and eagerly sweeping away his ancestor's bowling green and scented rose garden in favour of a Rococo design for his grounds. This style repudiated the earlier formal gardens favoured by aristocrats coming back from their European journeys who copied the linear lines and manicured lay-outs of Dutch, French and Italian gardens.

The main and most famous proponent of the new English 'look' in the mid-eighteenth century was Lancelot 'Capability' Brown whose sinuous paths across expanses of smooth green sward were linked with artfully placed trees, streams and lakes looking as if nature herself had placed them there. It was Brown who cleverly installed the 'ha-ha' in many of his schemes whereby an unseen sunken fence at the edge of a garden allows the eye to travel to 'views that have no bounds'. A device that also made it appear as if everything in sight belonged to the householder. Brown worked on almost two hundred gardens including Blenheim Palace, Chatsworth, Ragley Hall and Longleat for the grandest clientele. Inevitably he attracted criticism and controversy both 'at the time' and particularly after his death in 1783 when his work was seen as bland and incapable of engendering the thrill of the sublime that real nature could provide.

'They gradually ascended for half a mile, and then found themselves at the top of a considerable eminence, where the wood ceased, and the eye was instantly caught by Pemberley House, situated on the opposite side of a valley...it was a large, handsome, stone building, standing well on rising ground, and backed by a ridge of high woody hills' *Pride and Prejudice*

Elizabeth Bennett's description in *Pride and Prejudice* of the magnificent grounds at Pemberley show that she rejected this confected landscape and preferred the picturesque wildness praised by Gilpin which worked *with* nature and its 'rude views'. Henry Austen remarked that Jane was a 'warm and judicious admirer of landscape both in nature and on canvas'.

A view taken from the Pleasure Grounds of Adlestrop Park and its Cedar of Lebanon.

Photo by kind permission of Geoffrey Smith

The large lake at the far end of the grounds of Adlestrop Park in earlier days, looking as Humphry Repton intended.

Photo by kind permission of Ralph Price

The gabled old seventeenth-century rectory at Adlestrop, where Jane Austen stayed with her cousin, the Reverend Thomas Leigh, on at least three occasions. This may be the inspiration for the fictional Thornton Lacey in Mansfield Park.

Photo taken in the early twentieth century. By kind permission of David Hanks, Cotswold Images

The church of St Mary Magdalene in Adlestrop where Jane Austen worshipped on her visits to the village. On a high bank, the churchyard overlooks the old rectory.

Photo by kind permission of Geoffrey Smith

The bottom of Main Street in the village before it was tarmacked, showing the whiteness of the limestone road and traditional Cotswold cottages. The distant figure is a woman collecting water from the village pump.

Photo taken in the early twentieth century by kind permission of David Hanks, Cotswold Images

The top of Adlestrop Main Street showing the thatched roof of the current Post Office, a true cottage ornée.

Photo taken in the early twentieth century by kind permission of David Hanks, Cotswold Images

A watercolour sketch design by Humphry Repton for a decorative bath house and seat in the flower gardens of Adlestrop Park.

By kind permission of the Shakespeare Birthplace Trust

The shallow pool that lay below the bath house with the steps down to it, fed by spring water, leading to a cascading stream in the grounds of Adlestrop Park, laid out by Humphry Repton to look as natural as possible.

Photo by kind permission of Geoffrey Smith

Top left: *Jane Austen's great-grandfather, Theophilus Leigh (1643-1724), whose second wife, Mary, was the sister of the Duke of Chandos. Old-fashioned and strict he fathered twelve children at Adlestrop Park, among them Jane Austen's grandfather, Thomas.*

Top right: *The Honourable Mary Leigh, the sister of Edward, the fifth Lord Leigh, who was declared a lunatic in 1774. She gave church livings to James Austen and Edward Cooper and her death in 1806 allowed the Adlestrop Leighs to inherit Stoneleigh Abbey.*

Bottom left: *James Leigh (1724-1774), who employed the gothic architect, Sanderson Miller, to transform the façade of Adlestrop Park and enclosed all the common land.*

Bottom right: *James Henry Leigh (1765-1823) as a small boy still dressed in girl's clothes. He lived at Stoneleigh Abbey with his wife, the daughter of Lord Saye & Sele.*

All images by kind permission of Stoneleigh Abbey. Photography by Geoffrey Smith

Top left: *A portrait believed to be of Jane's cousin, the Reverend Thomas Leigh (1734-1813), as a young man. He was vicar at Adlestrop for over fifty years until he inherited Stoneleigh Abbey in 1806.*

By kind permission of Stoneleigh Abbey. Photograph Geoffrey Smith

Top right: *Elizabeth Wentworth (1696-1788), aunt and benefactress of James Leigh. Her romantic story of a clandestine marriage and secret fidelity to her husband may have suggested both the name of Captain Wentworth and one of the themes of* Persuasion.

By kind permission of Stoneleigh Abbey

Below: *Humphry's Repton watercolour aping the style of Claude from his Red Book for Stoneleigh Abbey. It shows the 'before' view of the south front being staked out under the direction of Repton standing with his umbrella in the foreground.*

By kind permission of Stoneleigh Abbey

Left: *A juxtaposition of the medieval gatehouse at Stoneleigh Abbey as seen from the West Wing. The difference in style was admired by Repton.*

Below: *The huge face of the West Wing at Stoneleigh Abbey in the English Baroque idiom, built in the 1720s by Francis Smith for the third Lord Leigh. The number of windows amazed Mrs Austen on her visit in 1806.*

Both by kind permission of Stoneleigh Abbey. Photographs Geoffrey Smith

The iconic old Great Western Railway sign for Adlestrop station. The bench has a brass plaque inscribed with the Edward Thomas poem 'Adlestrop'. It is the first thing visitors today see as they come into the village.

Photo by kind permission of Geoffrey Smith

The graceful Coade Stone urn to commemorate Warren Hastings (1732-1818) at Daylesford Church. He greatly admired Jane Austen's novels and had many connections to both the Austens and the Leigh families.

Photo by kind permission of Geoffrey Smith

The grounds were also a tribute to Darcy who used his own good taste in their creation, rather than employing an improver. In the novel Elizabeth mischievously tells her sister when she changed her mind about Darcy: '...I believe it must date from my first seeing his beautiful grounds at Pemberley.'

In *Mansfield Park*, Edmund also prefers to act on his own initiative stating: 'I should not put myself into the hands of an improver. I would rather have an inferior degree of beauty, of my own choice, and acquired progressively.' But Mary Crawford is of the opposite view, '...I should be most thankful to any Mr Repton who would undertake it, and give as much beauty as he could for my money'.

It was Humphry Repton who would take over Capability Brown's position as the nation's most eminent improver to the people of fashion and he also became pilloried and satirised. Jane Austen was not the only person to notice him in her fiction. In *Headlong Hall* Thomas Love Peacock caricatured him as Marmaduke Milestone who arrives with 'a portfolio under his arm' (his famous Red Book) and is described as 'a picturesque landscape gardener of the first celebrity, who was not without hopes of persuading Squire Headlong to put his romantic pleasure-grounds under a process of improvement'. Mr Milestone begs the squire to:

> ...accord me your permission to wave the wand of enchantment over your grounds. The rocks shall be blown up, the trees shall be cut down...Pagodas and Chinese bridges, gravel walks and shrubberies, bowling greens, canals, and lumps of larch, shall rise upon its ruins.

Repton began his career in 1788 and was soon successful, employed by great patrons such as the Duke of Portland and William Pitt the Younger. On his engraved visiting card he gave himself the title of 'Landscape Gardener' and showed himself surveying a lake surrounded by woodland with a tower in the distance. Like Gilpin whom he much admired, Repton was a talented water colourist and hit on a novel way to entice his gilded patrons. After he had studied the place in question he would deliver his Red Book – so-called because many were sumptuously bound in red morocco leather. Inside, written sections titled 'Character' 'Situation' etc were illustrated with his delightful watercolours with ingenious overlays showing the 'before' – a prosaic unimproved view, but when the flap of the overlay was lifted, the 'after' scene underneath was revealed demonstrating how Repton would enhance and transform the landscape. Sir Walter Scott described this as 'a raree show omitting only the magnifying glass & substituting his red book for the box and strings'.

As she was working on the final draft of *Pride and Prejudice* in 1811, Jane Austen was also writing *Mansfield Park* where two chapters examine some of the issues of improvements – both in the physical and moral sense. Many writers on Jane Austen believe that these chapters were influenced by her knowledge of Repton's work at Stoneleigh Abbey forgetting perhaps that her visits to Adlestrop over the years must

'I never saw a place so altered in my life. I told Smith I did not know where I was.'
Mansfield Park

also have played their part. Even before Repton came to the village Jane's mother and the Leighs would have pointed out to her the many alterations they had made.

Originally the village formed a semi-circle facing southwest across a village green of three and a half acres with the brook beyond it. It stretched from Marsh Bridge in the northwest where the road from Evenlode crossed the brook, to the church, parsonage and Adlestrop Park where a road came in from Daylesford.[7] It must have resembled the handsome large green still to be seen at neighbouring Broadwell. In 1767 the Revd Thomas Leigh enclosed this green, known as the Cross Green, with his brother's consent, so he could include it in his own grounds at the parsonage and then built roads around this new area: the eastern side became the village street and the road between Evenlode and Daylesford was taken alongside the right hand side of the parish brook. This effectively diverted traffic from the heart of the village making it more secluded and private – something that one can be thankful for now but perhaps not necessarily welcome to the villagers two hundred years ago. A new road was made between the north side of the village to connect and shorten the route from Marsh Bridge to Schoolers Lane which then climbed steeply to join the turnpike at Norton Gap. So now the houses were arranged around a triangle of roads which remain today.

At the parsonage itself Revd Leigh had already shown his awareness of exploiting the outside country views by moving his front door and having his principal rooms facing the pretty valley previously obscured by an unsightly farmhouse. A few years later when Blundels Field was enclosed and became part of his land in his role as rector, he added this to the Cross Green area and laid 'near three acres of ground under water' creating a

> '...having reached the ornamental part of the premises, consisting of a walk around two sides of a meadow...she was sufficiently recovered to think it prettier than any pleasure-ground she had ever been in before...' *Northanger Abbey*

lovely small lake to add to his vista. Now he had a 'Pleasure Ground' to rival his brother's. To make the short walk from the house down the lawns and through the shrubbery to saunter around the lake was a treat for a fine day. (see page 110)

A list of the distances to footpaths and roads once they had been improved in Adlestrop exists in Revd Leigh's handwriting and is dated 1798. He notes for example that the new turnpike road is 'Farther by 2.45 but more commodious being wider and easier of ascent'. I presume the distances are taken from the rectory to the roads in question – his calculations appear to be

'...my idea of moving the path to Langham, of turning it more to the right that it may not cut through the home meadow, I cannot conceive any difficulty. I should not attempt it, if it were to be the means of inconvenience to the Highbury people...' *Mr Knightley to his brother John. Emma*

in the old measurement of a chain which is 20.12 m or 22 yards. The 'Old footway between Hide End and Conygree Lane, to Chastleton' is 'Farther by 3.38 but much more commodious being over much drier ground'. A hand drawn map shows the old roads and footpaths compared to the new ones.[8]

The documents speak of the Turnpike road 'leading from Stow towards Chiping [sic] Norton through the said New Inclosure shall be and Remain upon the same spot it Now Goes (Next Dailsford Grounds) and be of the Bredth of Sixty feet in Every post thereof'. A road sixty-foot wide (approximately eighteen metres) included the wide grass verges characteristic of many country roads today and also allowed space for carriages to manoeuvre around pot holes and muddy patches.[9] For a lesser highway the width would be 40ft; for other carriage roads and bridleways a width of 20ft was advised and public footpaths around 4ft. In 1796 two Justices of the Peace attended a petty sessions at Adlestrop on the question of 'diverting and turning certain Highways & Foot Paths in the Parish' sets out that all this is to be done, 'to make ye same nearer & more commodious to the Publick'. This is how the advantages to the grounds of the Leighs were obviously presented to the magistrates. They note that 'all of the aforesaid new turnpike road highways and footway lead thro' the grounds of James Henry Leigh Esq. whose consent to the same we have received by writing under his hand & seal'.

To the north and east of Marsh Bridge, the old mill and a group of cottages were demolished at the end of the eighteenth century but new buildings went up too such as Manor Farm House and Lower Farm House. In a later codicil dated 1803 the same magistrates give their consent to all the changes with the proviso that the Revd Thomas Leigh and all his successors will have 'a free passage...for persons horses & carriages to & from the Parsonage House at Adlestrop thro the meadows or grass grounds belonging to James Henry Leigh' and also a free passage to Parsonage Farm [now Hillside Farm].

When all this work was going on, presumably carried out by village labourers and local builders, it must have caused a great disturbance to anyone living there or visiting and among those visitors was Jane Austen who would have seen all these alterations. No doubt the letters between the Austens and Elizabeth Leigh at the Parsonage also carried news of the upheavals. Jane had a

'...for three months we were all dirt and confusion, without a gravel walk to step on, or a bench fit for use...' *Mansfield Park*

ringside seat during her three forays into Gloucestershire in 1794, 1799 and 1806 to see the theory of the Picturesque being put into practice. While the roadworks were taking place at one end of the village, James Henry Leigh was adding to his garden too, and the lengths he had to go achieve his aims were considerable as can be seen from an extraordinary document in the Gloucestershire archives.[10] In 1799 James Henry Leigh with his uncle, the Reverend Thomas Leigh petitioned the Bishop of Gloucester so that part of Adlestrop churchyard could be incorporated into the garden of Adlestrop Park.

The area is recorded with great precision, it was not used for burial and was formerly a mill pond at the top of the parsonage kitchen garden. The Mill Pond can be seen on the 1759 map and Samuel Driver plan of Addlesthorp Town.[11] The reason given for this request was that it would be 'granted to him and added to the garden or Pleasure Grounds to make the same more commodius'. The directions are precise mentioning village landmarks such as the Great Old Elm Tree and various villagers' cottages and gardens belonging to William Naish,

Anthony Gibson and Widow Gardiner.

To underline the validity of his petition James Henry Leigh asked no fewer than six prominent men in the district to come and see the 'Truth of what he is saying': the Rector of Upper Slaughter, the Rector of Bourton-on-the-Hill, George Talbot of Upper Guiting, Richard Hippisley of Stow and the Rector of Stow, and Clerk of Upper Slaughter. All these good gentlemen appear to have fallen in with James Henry Leigh's plans and stated that the 'exchanges of Parcels of land…would be in the least prejudical to present or future rectors and inhabitants'. The opinions of the villagers were not canvassed.

In return for the land James Henry was prepared to spend a lot of his own money to:

> enclose the church yard with a substantial and good stonewall and make a much more commodious and convenient Church Road and way to Parish Church raising and fencing the road with posts from Widow Barrington's Cottage to Gate of Church.

This, the document adds, 'would be attended with Great Expense to James Henry Leigh'.

The building of the stone wall was also possibly designed to shut out the gloomy sight of the churchyard and its gravestones from the house and today you can see the same high stone wall between the churchyard and Adlestrop Park. An ornate iron gateway stands in the wall on the south side of the church, probably erected at this time and fashioned by the village blacksmith, which would have given direct entry to the grounds of the house and allowed its residents a direct and easy route to their devotions. One might have thought that these upheavals were

'…we should have carried on the garden wall, and made the plantation to shut out the churchyard, just as Dr Grant has done.' *Mansfield Park*

enough for the Leighs but around 1800 both brothers must have been dissatisfied with their handiwork because the Reverend decided to call in Humphry Repton to undertake an unusual project – to unite the improved rectory gardens and those of Adlestrop Park's thereby improving the views of each.

Unfortunately there is no existing Red Book nor correspondence between Repton and his Adlestrop patrons so we cannot see his plans clearly and much of his vision has been obscured and altered by other designers and neglect over the centuries. One tantalising survival of Repton's plans does exist however in the form of a charming little handpainted watercolour about the size of a modern postcard showing a Bath House and Seat approached by a winding path in the flower garden at Adlestrop Park.[12] It shows a small building looking like a tent with painted green spars and trellises. A short passage leads from the main structure to a beswagged exit in front of a pool above a little cascade tumbling into a lake. A waiting lady in white muslin stands at its entrance. Careful plans for its construction are on another document and although the structure has long gone the shallow base for the pool that was in front of it can still be seen and the stone steps leading to it. There was a strong fashion in the eighteenth century for the health benefits of bathing not only at spas and the seaside but outdoors in cold water. In September 1804 Jane Austen herself enjoyed bathing in the sea at Lyme Regis.[13] Plunge pools and bath houses such as this one at Adlestrop were created all over the country from

'I must try to do something with it,' said Mr Rushworth, 'but I do not know what. I hope I shall have some good friend to help me.'

'Your best friend upon such an occasion,' said Miss Bertram, calmly, 'would be Mr Repton, I imagine.'

'That is what I was thinking of. As he has done so well by Smith, I think I had better have him at once. His terms are five guineas a day.'

Mansfield Park

the grotto pool at Stourhead to a plunge pool at Painswick in south Gloucestershire. They were sited outside so that the bathing could be part of an exercise regime after riding or walking in the grounds. Their situation was also believed to be important, a setting in a beautiful landscape or garden such as the one in Adlestrop was believed to have a further positive effect on the bath's curative properties.[14] All in all this pretty bath house confirms the fashionable aspirations of the Leighs and must have been a talking point with the Austens.

One of the first matters Repton attended to was the recent and troublesome incorporation of the mill pond into the grounds from the churchyard. His ideas were explained in one of his influential books published in 1803 when his scheme for Adlestrop was still fresh in his mind. The Revd Leigh had a copy of this work, *Observations on the Theory and Practice of Landscape Gardening,* in his library, purchased perhaps directly from its author at the reduced price of two guineas – its advertised price was four guineas. In a passage about another garden, Thorseby Park in Nottinghamshire, Repton noted:

It may perhaps be objected, that to introduce rock scenery in this place would be unnatural; but if this artifice be properly executed, no eye can discover the illusion; and it is only in by such deceptions that art can imitate the most pleasing works of nature. By the help of such illusion we may see the interesting struggles of the babbling brook, which soon after "spreads into a liquid plain, then stands unmov'd, Pure as the expanse of heaven."

After this quotation from *Paradise Lost* he goes on to remark:

This idea has been realized in the scenery at ADLESTROP, where a small pool, very near the house, was supplied by a copious stream of clear water. The cheerful glitter of this little mirror, although on top of a hill, gave pleasure to those who had never considered how much it lessened the place, by attracting the eye and preventing its range over the lawn and the falling ground beyond.

This pool has now been removed; a lively stream of water has been led through a flower-garden, where its progress down the hill is occasionally obstructed by ledges of rocks, and after a variety of interesting circumstances it falls into a lake at a considerable distance, but in full view of both the mansion and the parsonage, to each of which it makes a delightful, because a natural feature in the landscape.[15]

An 1815 guide describes it:

Among its picturesque features may be ranked a small stream, which, in its progress down a hill, has its current checked by ledges of rocks, and at length falls into a lake at some distance from the house.[16]

Now very little of this arrangement is in full view. A small pool exists at the base of the garden of Adlestrop Park feeding the stream which, in turn, feeds the two lakes. The larger lake can hardly be seen from either house due to the growth of trees although there is still a lovely view to the little lake from the old parsonage. The 'little lake' has recently been dredged and restored to its former glory but is, I stress, completely private. The large lake 'at a considerable

'... in front, a stream of some natural importance was swelled into greater, but without any artificial appearance. Its banks were neither formal nor falsely adorned.' *Pride and Prejudice*

distance' – about a ten minute walk from the Park, is shaped like the bowl of a ladle and freshened by the streams above it which never dry up. A short stretch of river by the side of the meadow is fenced off from the public with ugly barbed wire and the lake itself is now used by a local fishing club and is also private. Early photographs show how pleasantly the lake once blended into an attractive scene with cattle grazing right up to the water's edge. As recently as the 1960s there was a wonderful circular walk from the rectory to the lake via a broad gravelled path enclosed with iron fences down the right hand side of the garden to a shingled wooden boathouse on the Little Lake, passing over a decorative wooden bridge to follow the side of the large lake before returning back to the rectory grounds by the side of the present bridleway. This arcadian pathway may have been originally put in place by Thomas Leigh and was unfortunately thoughtlessly grassed over, the boathouse demolished and the fencing removed. This alteration also helped to mask Repton's original vision that the two houses should share the beauties of the pleasure grounds while still being quite separate. Perhaps because of its present isolation the lake has a curious still atmosphere due to the surrounding mature trees that are mirrored in the opaque waters. In the summer the edges are threaded with yellow flags, meadowsweet and glistening white water lilies lie on the lake's surface. Swans, moorhens, herons, coots and mallards enjoy the lake and there is even a terrapin which basks in the sun on a jutting tree root on hot days. In the winter the water freezes frequently. It is a secretive place where one expects to see some Waterhouse nymphs instead of anglers who sit patiently hoping for a catch of the huge pike that swim in its depths.

Repton's 'lively stream' and cascade are completely hidden within shrubbery and woods as the water flows swiftly down behind the stone wall by the current bridleway just beyond the church. As to rocks and ledges only traces of these remain. A few clumps of Harts Tongue ferns and exquisite carpets of light mauve wild anemone have survived the years but otherwise laurel, holly and yew saplings and bramble bushes have colonised the area. To get an idea of how the walk by the stream would have looked one can see the beautiful Stream

Garden at Sezincote, near Moreton in Marsh, which aped the gentle rock ledges and cascade at Adlestrop and has been restored and kept up.

The old road through the park was now solely for the use of the Leighs and the rest of the traffic went a longer way round. The park, while not as large as Mr Rushworth's friend, Smith's, is a very attractive place to enjoy this view:

> Smith has not much above a hundred acres altogether in his grounds, which is little enough, and makes it more surprising that the place can have been so improved...there have been two or three fine old trees cut down that grew too near the house, and it opens the prospect amazingly. The approach *now* is one of the finest in the country. You see the house in the most surprising manner

Today the faint line of this road can easily be seen joining the current path as a line across the cricket ground when the weather is dry. In the grounds of the Park the line continues across the present lawn to end up in front of the pillared entrance. One of Repton's hallmarks was that the approach to a house should not be through a straight avenue of trees, nor ramble through the grounds, but it 'should be presented in a pleasing point of view'. In this idea he was quite right but today only a walker coming from the large lake or lower road on what is now a public bridleway will see this magnificent tableau of the stone gables of Adlestrop Park with a Cedar of Lebanon in front rising above a lawn which appears to fall naturally into a meadow dotted with clumps of trees, invariably grazed by a large flock of sheep and lambs. There is another entrance from the main road to the house and also one from the village, neither of which has any dramatic or picturesque quality.

The legacy that Jane Austen's cousins left to the lay-out and landscape of Adlestrop is considerable. None of these changes could have occurred without substantial funds which they held onto by exercising thrift and good management and were also lucky enough to inherit. Their energy and taste are to be admired. But there was a greater project impending for the Leighs of Adlestrop which was to have unpleasant ramifications for Jane Austen. Nothing in her life could bring the questions of family, money and fairness into sharper focus than the issues surrounding the inheritance of that great prize, Stoneleigh Abbey.

CHAPTER SEVEN

Family Quarrels: The Fight for Stoneleigh

'We must not all expect to be individually lucky…the luck of one member of the family is luck to all.' **The Watsons**

In 1806, thirty-two years after Edward, the fifth Lord Leigh of Stoneleigh Abbey was declared a lunatic, his sister Mary, who had been designated a life tenant of the estate, died. Edward's death without a male heir also meant that the peerage granted to the family by Charles I died with him. What did it mean for Jane so recently bereft of her own father? Surely it meant fresh hope that the Austen money problems would be alleviated in the share-out of the inheritance. And for the Leighs at Adlestrop it heralded an immediate upheaval. The senior branch of the family was returning to its roots.

Edward Leigh himself had died in 1786 at the age of forty-four leaving a host of bequests in his will, which had been signed long before his sanity deserted him. As already mentioned he had donated generously to his old college at Oxford, Oriel – all his mathematical instruments and the entire library at the house apart from the Stoneleigh Ledger Book and manuscripts relating to the medieval abbey. His funeral was a

'…the said Edward Lord Leigh…is a Lunatic of unsound Mind and that he doth not enjoy lucid intervals so as to be sufficient for the Government of himself his Manors, Messuages, Lands, Tenements Goods and Chattels'[1]

solemn one reflecting his rank: the procession was impressive – led by four mutes followed by the leading mourners, fifty tenants, twelve underbearers, pages and attendants. Six horses drew the hearse followed by three coaches carrying mourners and Edward's personal coach with his coat of arms on the side – now empty.[2]

His coffin draped with crimson velvet with an inscription in silver plate was placed in the family vault in the church at Stoneleigh.[3]

A touching prayer written by his elder sister Mary in about 1775 shows a little of the anguish she and the family must have felt over his mental breakdown:

> O Lord look down from Heaven, in much pity and compassion, upon thy afflicted servant, who is not able to now look up to thee, hear O most merciful Father my Prayers on his behalf, and preserve him from doing any harm to himself or to any other: be pleased to remove all frightfull imaginations far from him, and if it be the blessed will, O our God restore him to his reason and understanding, so will we all give thanks to thee for ever and ever. Amen.[4]

As a life tenant of Stoneleigh, the Hon. Mary Leigh had enjoyed her position in society. Not only was she given £20,000 but her annual income was about £13,000. How many Austens and Leighs would have been waiting for news of her demise? Did they keep their fingers crossed that she did not marry and provide an heir? Like Lady Lucas in *Pride and Prejudice* whose daughter Charlotte accepts the hand of Mr Collins, the destined legatee of the Bennet's house: 'Lady Lucas began directly to calculate with more interest than the matter had ever excited before, how many years longer Mr Bennet was likely to live...'

There is much evidence that the Hon. Mary was a kindly

woman and tried to help her extended family during her lifetime. A brief pen-portrait of her exists demonstrating her good intentions and a few eccentric traits. This was written down in the early twentieth century by a family descendant, Agnes Leigh, presumably relying on family letters, anecdote and hearsay. It appears at the back of the other Mary Leigh's history before a series of handwritten letters carefully pasted in that passed between the Hon. Mary and 'her man of business Mr Joseph Hill':

> Of a very short stature and rather plain of feature she lived a somewhat retired life and never married. It used to be said that she disliked being looked at and that the village people had orders not to look at her as she passed but the letters certainly show that she mixed in company, and went to Cheltenham exc. [Cheltenham Race Week]. A tradition in the Craven family says that she was attached to the Lord Craven of her day and used to watch for his coming. Upon her death the Rev Thomas Leigh first succeeded to the estates but he presently made an arrangement with the Head of the family…and returned to his peaceful existence at Adlestrop Rectory… The late Lord Leigh was mentally afflicted during the last years of his life, and the worthy lady whose death we record was not unmarked by some eccentricities, but of the most harmless nature…She was buried as she had requested in the clothes she wore at the time of her death – a handsome silk gown, a hoop, a cap with rich lace ….[5]

Mary stayed at Stoneleigh Abbey during the summer when she would entertain her friends and family. In the area she was known for her generosity and charity towards the poor. When autumn arrived she would be found taking the waters and enjoying the social life of either Bath or Cheltenham Spa accompanied by her long-standing friends Mrs Hale and Mrs

Herbert. In the winter, as the Season began she lived mainly in London at Grove House in Kensington Gore. This was just outside the centre but still sufficiently close to allow her to partake in all that smart society could offer.[6]

Most of her extant letters concern the business of the Stoneleigh estates. The Austen family connection was well known to her and she was eager to help them. In 1792 she gave James Austen, Jane's eldest brother, a church living that was in her gift, as this letter to Joseph Hill, about a living falling vacant in the village of Cubbington shows:

> Sir,
> I am very much obliged by your reminding me of Mr Austin [sic] & I think I am inclined to offer him the Living.... I beg yours & Mrs Hills acceptance of some French beans and mushrooms that came last night....[7]

A month later she wrote again, worrying that the rectory in Cubbington 'is left in a deplorable state...could I consistently make it comfortable... I should suppose all the inside must want a thorough cleaning'. It was up to the patron of the living or its incumbent to keep a rectory shipshape and never up to the church. There were often arguments about 'dilapidations' and the relationship between Mrs Norris and Dr Grant got off to a bad start over this very issue.

'Dr Grant and Mrs Norris were seldom good friends; their acquaintance had begun in dilapidations.'
Mansfield Park

In the event James did become vicar at Cubbington but was an absentee one and then he also took up the post of perpetual curate at Hunningham in 1805 (also at the Hon. Mary Leigh's disposal). James enjoyed the benefits of both these sinecures throughout his life while he was living in Hampshire, first as curate at Deane and then as rector at Steventon. Cubbington and Hunningham are a just a few miles from Stoneleigh and are now satellite villages of Leamington Spa. The Hon. Mary Leigh also endowed Jane's cousin, the sermon-writer Edward Cooper, with the living at Hamstall Ridware in Staffordshire, which was where the Austens were en route to on their landmark 1806 journey from Bath. She was also godmother to the Cooper's first daughter, Isabella Mary; in her will she left a legacy of an annuity of £200 for the care of Mrs Austen's 'imbecile' brother (Jane's uncle) – perhaps out of her first-hand experience of her brother's mental illness.[8]

The *Warwick and Warwickshire Advertiser* was well informed enough to note the Hon. Mary Leigh's death in its 5 July issue and report who would be the new landlord – naturally a matter of great interest to the locals: 'Lady Mary Leigh's death recorded at Kensington Gore on Wednesday Last. She is succeeded in her estates and possessions by the Rev. Thomas Leigh of Adlestrop.'

The funeral took place at Stoneleigh on 14 July and the *Warwick and Warwickshire Advertiser* now added more information to its earlier note on the inheritance:

> On Monday last, the funeral of the late Honourable Mary Leigh attended by a numerous and respectable tenantry…. she has by her last will settled all her estates upon that branch of the Leigh family which descended from that second son of Sir Thomas Leigh, Lord Mayor of London, at the accession of Queen Elizabeth…. The Revd. Thomas Leigh, James Leigh Perrot, and James Henry Leigh, Esq. of Adlestrop, and his issue male

It is no wonder that wills, entails and inheritance are major themes in Jane Austen. The long wait for the unravelling of the Stoneleigh affair had begun when she was a child and she must have grown up with the knowledge of it during any discussions about family assets. *Pride and Prejudice* hinges on the saga of the entail on Mr Bennet's estate, a binding legality which made it imperative that his five daughters should contract good marriages, otherwise they and their mother would be left both homeless and almost penniless in the event of their father's death. The sub-plot in *Pride and Prejudice* also hinges on Wickham's false denigration of Mr Darcy for failing to carry out the wishes of Mr Darcy's father who 'bequeathed me the next presentation of the best living in his gift', and blaming the will for not spelling these out clearly:

> There was such an informality in the terms of the bequest
> as to give me no hope from law. A man of honour could not
> have doubted the intention, but Mr Darcy chose to doubt
> it – or to treat it as a merely conditional recommendation.

Confusion in the case of Stoneleigh was compounded because the Hon. Mary Leigh made several wills in her lifetime naming first that the lands should be put in trust to the eldest representative of the Leigh senior line – that is to the Reverend Thomas Leigh for his life, then to James Leigh Perrot of Scarlets for life, a further life tenancy to James Henry Leigh of Adlestrop and then to his heirs. [9] A further condition of her wills was that all the life tenants were to reach an agreement within six months of her death, 'It being my wish to prevent any Contest concerning the property...'.[10] The will was described as 'vague' by Joseph Hill and was a legal minefield causing litigation from claimants all over England for many years. As we have seen in Chapter Two, James Leigh Perrot had already attempted to stake a claim in the 1780s and had been rebuffed but the issue could not be ignored any longer.

The Austens' closest relative amongst these three possible contenders for the bulk of the inheritance was Jane's uncle on her mother's side, James Leigh Perrot. He had already been enriched as a young man by the Perrot family and could reasonably be expected to disperse some of his gains to his widowed sister and her unmarried daughters. Jane, Cassandra and her mother had stayed with the Leigh Perrots very recently in Bath and he and his wife were well aware of their straitened circumstances.

It was a coincidence that Mary Leigh died on 2 July, the same day that the Austens had finally said goodbye to Bath. Mrs Austen, Jane and Cassandra were with their bosom friend, Martha Lloyd, on the first leg of their journey to Clifton in Bristol. Jane left Bath with a feeling of great relief which she referred to later as a memorable time: 'It will be two years tomorrow since we left Bath for Clifton, with what happy feelings of Escape!'[11] The Austens' sojourn at Bath had not been a success – her father had died there leaving his widow and daughters moving from one set of rented rooms to another, always forced to choose the most economical. They were reliant on any hand-outs from the Austen sons and were grateful for Francis' invitation to them to share his Southampton home when he returned from his honeymoon. To kill time the three ladies were taking this extended trip to see their relations. 1806 was a pivotal juncture for Jane Austen, none of her novels had yet been published, she had no marital prospects and no fixed home. It is worth recording here the best account we have of the writing schedule of Jane's novels penned by Cassandra and reflect on how much she had accomplished but, at this stage, had received no public acknowledgment apart from encouragement within her own family. It also shows how the writing of different drafts overlapped each other and the long gap between the first three novels written at Steventon and the last three written at Chawton. How much she concentrated on her work in the intervening restless years can only be guessed at.

First Impressions begun in Oct. 1796
Finished in Augt 1797. Published
afterwards, with alterations & contractions
under the Title of Pride & Prejudice.
Sense & Sensibility begun Nov. 1797
I am sure that something of the

same story & characters had been
Written earlier & called Elinor & Marianne
   Mansfield Park, begun somewhere
About Feb[y] 1811 — Finished soon after
June 1813
   Emma – begun Jan[y] 21st 1814, finished
March 29th 1815
   Persuasion begun Aug[t] 8th 1815
Finished Aug[t] 6th 1816

On the verso
North-hanger Abbey was written
About the years 98 & 99
                 C.E.A. [12]

The Austens parted with Martha at Clifton in Bristol and stayed there for a few weeks before carrying on with their long-arranged visit to Adlestrop. They arrived having presumably received letters along the way telling them of the Hon. Mary Leigh's demise and were probably anxious to hear everything first hand from their cousins at Adlestrop Rectory. Revd Thomas Leigh had returned to Adlestrop on 17 July after the funeral engaging in a daily round of letters with Joseph Hill about the inheritance. Thomas' attempts to pin down James Leigh Perrot on a settlement for the Austens and Coopers must have been heightened by their forthcoming arrival.

James Leigh Perrot was vociferous in his claim on the Stoneleigh inheritance, aided and abetted by his wife, Jane. Within forty-eight hours of the Hon. Mary Leigh's death he was already in London and wrote to his wife at 4 o'clock on Friday, 4 July. In the letter he said that on his arrival in London he had dined with Joseph Hill and they had discussed all 'those materially interested in the Landed Property' [i.e. Stoneleigh] which included himself, Thomas Leigh and James Henry Leigh. He went on to elaborate the situation, being mainly irritated by the fact that Thomas Leigh had gone to Stoneleigh instead of coming up to London to hear the reading of the will. This was quite unfair on his part as Thomas had been a visitor to Stoneleigh over many years and felt it up to him to sort out the many issues arising from the Hon. Mary Leigh's death at the Abbey itself – not least organising and attending the funeral and the interment of her body in the family vault at Stoneleigh church.

On the reading of the will it was revealed that Mary Leigh had named Joseph Hill and Thomas Leigh joint executors and residuary legatees. However Leigh Perrot informed his wife that: 'Mr Hill tells me that the Uncle and Nephew must and will act handsomely towards me.' James took away papers from this meeting to consult his wife on the matter while also proudly stating that he was rich enough and hardly needed any increase in his fortune, but he still held out for a huge annual payment in exchange for giving up any claim to the estate. Joseph Hill reported back to Thomas Leigh that 'Mrs Leigh Perrot was not present at the conversation but I believe her influence has great weight with his determination'. Leigh Perrot wanted an immediate payment of £20,000.

Joseph Hill then spent three days at his house in Wargrave coincidentally near to his neighbours, the Perrots, trying to thrash out a deal and writing daily missives to Adlestrop on his progress. The Reverend's main concern was that his nephew should be able to succeed him without delay after his own death and beat down Leigh Perrot's demand for £3,000 a year in lieu of the inheritance to an annuity of £2,000 during the lives of the Perrots calculated on 5 per cent interest on £20,000. The capital sum would only be paid when James Henry succeeded to the estate. The Reverend Leigh took into consideration, 'from my regard to Leigh Perrot and for the Cooper and Austen families, & to ensure to Mr L.P. the means of better providing for them who are so very numerous'.[13] It was this transaction which Jane Austen would later refer to as a 'vile compromise'.

Many biographers of Jane Austen assume that the Austens' visit to Stoneleigh was a spur of the moment decision taken on their arrival at Adlestrop in the first week of August but the correspondence shows that this was not the case. Letters also firmly contradict the accusation so often levelled at Thomas Leigh that he rushed off in an unseemly manner to Stoneleigh to stake a firm claim on a shaky inheritance. Nothing could be further from the truth and he waited at Adlestrop until the Austens arrived so he could accompany them to Stoneleigh, as not only

'…he would never condescend to sell…the Kellynch estate should be transmitted whole and entire, as he had received it.'
Persuasion

would it help them on their way to their final destination in Staffordshire, but also to share with them the splendours of the Abbey for a brief holiday. There may well have been some shrewd thinking on Mrs Austen's part in continuing her journey to her cousin at this crucial point, calculating that her very presence as a widow with two unmarried and portionless daughters would remind him of their penury just as he was coming into a fortune. From all accounts the Austens were never given a full picture of what was going on behind the scenes by any of the participants and it was this secrecy that caused so much anguish to Jane.

The matter of the will was still a pressing one in her letters two years later. In the summer of 1808 she wrote from Southampton:

'Mr Tho. Leigh is again in Town — or was very lately. Henry met with him last Sunday in St James's Church. — He owned being come up unexpectedly on Business— which we of course think can be only *one* business—& he came post from Adlestrop in one day, which — if it cd be doubted before—convinces Henry that he will live for ever.

This acerbic aside is a mark of the stress caused to her by the uncertainty of her own affairs. She went on to say:

> Mrs Knight [brother Edward's adoptive mother] is kindly anxious for our Good, & thinks Mr L.P. *must* be desirous for his *Family's* sake to have everything settled.–Indeed I do not know where we are to get our Legacy–but we will keep a sharp look-out.[14]

It appears that both the Coopers and the Austens were given the impression by the Leigh Perrots that they would pass on any money that came to them and this was certainly what the Reverend wanted. Joseph Hill endeavoured to ensure that the Leigh Perrots should give £8,000 out of the £20,000 to 'Mrs Austen's family and Mr Cooper's' but Mr Leigh Perrot only promised that 'he would make such provision himself, as he thought proper.' In the end nothing was, at this time, passed on to the Austens or Coopers by the wealthy Leigh Perrots and Jane put the blame at her aunt's door; her exasperation with the clandestine complications over the money is clear:

> Yes, The Stoneleigh Business is concluded...My Aunt says as little as may be on the subject by way of information & nothing at all by way of satisfaction...she reflects on Mr T. Leigh's dilatoriness, & looks about with great diligence & success for Inconvenience and Evil...not a word of arrears mentioned ... The amount of them is a matter of conjecture, & to my Mother a most interesting one; she cannot fix any time for their beginning, with any satisfaction to herself, but Mrs Leigh's death– and Henry's two Thousand pounds neither agrees with that period, nor any other...I did not like to own , our previous information of what was intended last July– and have therefore only said that if we could see Henry we might

hear many particulars, as I had understood that some confidential conversation had passed between him and Mr T.L. at Stoneleigh.[15]

Five years later and the matter is still one that rankles with her. After speaking of the death of Revd Thomas Leigh she goes on to say:

We are very anxious to know who will have the Living of Adlestrop, & where his excellent Sister will find a home for the remainder of her days. As yet she bears his Loss with fortitude, but she has always seemed so wrapt up in him, that I feel she must feel it dreadfully when the fever of Business is over.—There is another female sufferer on the occasion to be pitied. Poor Mrs L.P.—who would now have been Mistress of Stonleigh [sic] had there been none of that vile compromise which in good truth has never been allowed to be of much use to them—It will be a hard trial.[16]

Complications and injustices about wills and inheritances in *Sense and Sensibility* parallel the contrast between the riches of the Leigh Perrots and the poverty of the Austens. Mrs Dashwood and her three daughters are left on the edges of poverty when the Norland Estate passes to Mr Dashwood's son John (from a first marriage), who was already 'amply provided for by the fortune of his mother' and 'By his own marriage... he added to his wealth. To him therefore the succession to the Norland estate was

'Altogether, they will have five hundred a-year amongst them, and what on earth can four women want for more than that? —They will live so cheap! Their housekeeping will be nothing at all. They will have no carriage, no horses,and hardly any servants; they will keep no company, and can have no expences of any kind!'
Sense and Sensibility

not so really important as to his sisters; for their fortunes…
could be but small.' On his deathbed Mr Dashwood talked
to his son 'with all the strength and urgency which illness
could command, the interest of his mother-in-law and sisters.'
Naturally the young man promised his father 'to do everything
in his power to make them comfortable' repeating this to his
wife, 'It was my father's last request to me… that I should assist
his widow and daughters.' At the time he decides to give each
girl 'a thousand pounds a-piece… three thousand pounds! He
could spare so considerable a sum with little inconvenience.'
However under the influence of his wife, a woman characterised
as 'narrow-minded and selfish', his good intentions are
whittled away entirely and 'he finally resolved, that it would be
absolutely unnecessary, if not highly indecorous, to do more
for the widow and children of his father, than such kind of
neighbourly acts as his own wife pointed out.'

James Leigh Perrot continued to harass his Leigh cousins
about his pay-off. In 1813 he wrote a bad-tempered letter to
Revd Thomas Leigh at Adlestrop regarding the payment of Mr
James Henry Leigh's bond without suitable notice to himself:

If I had known your intention, I could have placed the
money out much to my satisfaction and greatly to my
advantage, but this opportunity I have now lost. How
could I have any suspicion that you meant to pay off the
Bond? I think I have reason to complain, as I must now be a
considerable loser; and I lent the £4000 to Mr James Henry
Leigh solely at your Request and not for any advantage to
myself; and I could at that time have placed it in the Funds
much better than I can now.

As I am writing, I will mention that Mr Wood two
years ago sent me from Leighton [Buzzard] for a Brace of
Pheasants, last year no Pheasant but a Brace of Hares, and
this year neither Partridge, Pheasant nor Hare. I think it of
no consequence whether I receive my game from Leighton

or no; but I was willing to mention it to you; that if Mr Wood did not send any to your other relations or Friends, you may not suppose it was owing to supplying me.

Mrs Leigh Perrot joins with me in best wishes to your good sister & yourself'[17]

An emollient reply came from the Reverend defending his payment of the bond but saying it can be delayed if Leigh Perrot wishes, also if he wants any game just to ask and reminding him that some time ago he had asked that Mr Wood should not send him any game. Although his reasonable reply shows no signs of age his handwriting has noticeably deteriorated.

Leigh Perrot also wrote to James Henry Leigh complaining that he only wants the interest on the bond and he is happy to let him have the money as long as he wants – discounting his uncle's (Thomas) idea of paying out the capital sum as the right thing to do. A flurry of letters between the Leigh's lawyer in London, Mr Mortimer who resided at the Albany, Thomas Leigh and Leigh Perrot on this subject continued. After the Reverend's death in June 1813 Leigh Perrot takes up the offensive again with James Henry Leigh in September:

I have no objection to your paying the 20000 £ at Christmas next into Messrs Hoare's House on my account. I received a letter last year from Mr Mortimer to inform me that upon Mr Chandos Leigh coming of Age the entail upon the Stoneleigh Property was intended to be cut off... when you and I settled the terms on which I gave up my chance of succession my intention was to be paid £3000 a year clear from all outgoings...Your uncle always added Property Tax... I never mentioned to him what a loser I was every year because all my friends assured me that when Mr Chandos Leigh was twenty one and the entail cut off (by which you will be empowered to cut down timber to so great an amount as to encrease your income exceedingly) you certainly would repay me the money so kept back, for though it might not be recoverable by Law, yet an intentional agreement between two gentlemen was undoubtedly binding.[18]

To a man as rich as he was, Leigh Perrot's grievances and whining for his last shilling no doubt added to the opprobrium the Austens and the Leighs felt towards him and his wife. The matter seems to have been resolved in 1813 with Leigh Perrot's letter of 19 October saying he can wait for his £24,000 until convenient and thanking James Henry for not deducting Property Tax. The present day value of this money would be considerable – some historians talk of a multiple of times 200 to translate this into contemporary values.[19] Compare this with Darcy's £10,000 a year, his Derbyshire seat and land plus a smart house in the capital or Bingley's inheritance of £100,000 but no land or property. Then look at the pitiful amount Mrs Austen, Jane and Cassandra had at their disposal after Mr Austen's death and before her brothers came to their aid – a mere £210 a year. A final twist in the saga occurred just months before Jane Austen's death in 1817. In early April she wrote to her brother Charles,

I am ashamed to say that the shock of my Uncle's Will brought on a relapse, & I was so ill on Friday & thought myself so likely to be worse that I could not but press for Cassandra's returning with Frank after the Funeral last night...I am the only one of the Legatees who has been so silly, but a weak Body must excuse weak nerves. [20]

James Leigh Perrot had died on 28 March at the age of 82 and since he had no heirs the Austen family were naturally hoping he would have remembered them in his will. The family were in a bad way financially – one on half-pay, Henry bankrupt and Edward Knight short of funds, so they must have all hoped for assistance. Henry's bank had collapsed in 1816 and his debts to the Exchequer were considerable and the sureties of his relatives and friends were now called in. Edward Knight and Leigh Perrot paid £21,000 in instalments between April 1816 and March 1817 (after Leigh Perrot's death his widow repaid a further £8,600).[21] Other members of the wider Austen family paid off other of the bank's debts — Jane herself lost £25.7.0 which she had on deposit at her brother's bank. The whole affair was public and humiliating for the family.[22] So it is no surprise that Jane should feel so devastated. It is typical of the importance given to family funerals that Cassandra had left her sister's sick bed and went to help their aunt in Berkshire, closely followed by James, Mary and Francis. However far from remembering his sister and her children James Leigh Perrot left everything to his wife for her life and placed Scarlets and his other properties at Bath at her disposal plus a large capital sum. He did however leave a considerable bequest (to be paid after his wife's death) to James Austen and his heirs and £1000 to each of Mrs Austen's children who might survive his wife. As none of these benefits would accrue for some time — in fact Mrs Leigh Perrot did not die until 1836 — Jane's anger is understandable. Jane's letter continued:

'I shall not be a poor old maid; and it is poverty only which makes celibacy contemptible to a generous public! A single woman with a very narrow income, must be a ridiculous, disagreeable old maid!...but a single woman, of good fortune, is always respectable, and may be as sensible and pleasant as anybody else'.
Emma

> My mother has borne the forgetfulness of *her* extremely well–her expectations for herself were never beyond the extreme of moderation, and she thinks with you that my Uncle always looked forward to surviving her...[she] heartily wishes that her younger children had more, and all her children something immediately...[23]

When Jane earned some money of her own from her books, her delight shines through – although she is careful to relay the information to her correspondents in a self-deprecating tone. In 1813 she writes to her brother Frank on HMS *Elephant:*

> You will be glad to hear that every Copy of S &S is sold & that it has bought me £140—besides the Copyright, if that shd ever be of any value.—I have now written myself into £250—which only makes me long for more.[24]

In the spring of her final year Jane had drawn up a note on her own earnings in 1817 apart from the £600 already earned from her pen:

<u>Profits of my Novels, over & above the £600 in the Navy Fives</u>

	£
Residue from the Ist Edit: of Mansfield Park,	
remaining in Henrietta S^t.–March 1816	13. .7 –
Rec^d. From Egerton, on 2^d Edit: of Sense & S–	
March 1816	12. .15 –
Feb^r.21.1817　　From Profits from Emma	38. .18 –
March 7. 1817　From Egerton – 2^d Edit: S & S	19. .13 –

On 27 April she who had written so much in her fiction and in her own correspondence about wills and inheritance, made her own last will and testament leaving nearly everything to her dear sister Cassandra:

> subject to the payment of my Funeral Expenses, & to a Legacy of £50. to my Brother Henry, and £50. to Mde Bijion – which I request may be paid as soon as convenient. And I appoint my said dear Sister the Executrix of this my last will & Testament.[25]

Jane died in Winchester on 18 July 1817.

CHAPTER EIGHT

The Real Sotherton?
Jane Austen at Stoneleigh Abbey

'Their road was through pleasant country; and Fanny, whose rides had never been extensive, was soon beyond her knowledge, and was very happy in observing all that was new, and admiring all that was pretty.' **Mansfield Park**

On 1 August 1806 the Revd Thomas Leigh planned to return to Stoneleigh with his sister, Elizabeth and the Austens, and Joseph Hill and his wife who had also come to stay at Adlestrop. He had earlier proposed this to Joseph Hill:

> It will be equally, if not more, convenient to me to accompany you next week to Stoneleigh, as it wd have been abt the 20th. We will therefore expect the pleasure of seeing you & Mrs Hill here before dinner on Monday next, & proceed ye next day to ye Abbey. Mrs & Miss Austens will be of ye party, & will then be so far on their road to Mr Cooper's whom they are going to visit at Hamstall. I wrote yesterday to Mr West to say yt we shd come to ye Abbey to dinner by 5 o'clock on Tuesday next, & desir'd him to have beds & every thing ready.[1]

This letter clearly confirms that the Rector's decision to go to Stoneleigh was a measured and planned-for event. The journey to the abbey from Adlestrop is about thirty miles. The route is the same today as it would have been for Jane Austen by coach and horses – on the turnpike to Stow on the Wold where the roads joins the ancient Fosse Way which makes its way north through Warwickshire. An hour by car, maybe six or seven for a coach – Jane would have been engaged throughout by enjoying the changing countryside which was all quite fresh to her. Like Fanny Price on her journey to Sotherton she was entertained: '…in observing the appearance of the country, the bearings of the roads, the difference of soil, the state of the harvest, the cottages, the cattle, the children…'[2]

The party left Adlestrop in two coaches, which allowed all seven of them to travel in comfort. One coach belonged to the Reverend, the other to the Hills'. Normally the men would have ridden on horseback and the women go by coach but as both the Hills and Jane's cousins were elderly they naturally preferred the option of a carriage. In *Mansfield Park* there were also seven travellers on the excursion to Sotherton, but Edmund chose to ride on horseback while the rest were comfortable in the Grants' barouche which Henry Crawford drove with Julia Bertram sitting

'…their approach to the capital freehold mansion, and ancient manorial residence of the family, with all its rights of Court-Leet and Court-Baron'
Mansfield Park

high up next to him enjoying the best of the views along the way. The barouche was preferred by Julia because it offered far more comfort than being 'box'd up three in a post-chaise in this weather'. The other objection to using the Bertram family carriage was that its varnish could be scratched on the narrow lanes causing upset to both the coachman and Sir Thomas Bertram. All our information on the Austens' stay at Stoneleigh comes from Jane's mother in her detailed letters to her daughter-in-law, Mary Austen, who then lived at Steventon Rectory.

Before the abbey is reached from the main roads, the wooded grounds of the Stoneleigh estate are all around.

Now the original estate has been broken up and its extensive landholdings shared between the 690 acres of parkland which remain as a setting for Stoneleigh Abbey, and over a thousand acres belonging to Stoneleigh Park, a company that hosts large open air events, festivals and trade fairs. This area was previously the site of the National Agriculture Centre which for many years hosted the Royal Show. The unspoilt village of Stoneleigh is some way from the abbey and its appearance and the approach to the mansion are echoed in *Mansfield Park* with a running commentary by Miss Bertram in the barouche directed at Mary Crawford:

> Here begins the village. Those cottages really are a disgrace. The church spire is reckoned remarkably handsome. I am glad the church is not so close to the Great House as often happens in old places. The annoyance of the bells must be terrible. There is the parsonage; a tidy-looking house, and I understand the clergyman and his wife are very decent people. Those are alm-houses built by some of the family...Now we are coming to the lodge gates; but we have nearly a mile through the park still. It is not ugly, you see, at this end; there is some fine timber, but the situation of the house is dreadful.[3]

Although the church at Stoneleigh does not have a spire, by the village green are five spacious alm houses built by the first Sir Thomas Leigh's widow, Dame Alice in 1594, each of red sandstone with a distinctive chimney stack.

While Mrs Austen's first impressions of the grounds could have been written by Catherine Morland herself:

> I had expected to find everything about the place very fine and all that, but I had no idea of its being so beautiful. I had figured to myself long Avenues dark Rookeries and Dismal Yew Trees, but there was no such melancholy things. The

Avon near the house amidst green meadows bounded by large and beautiful woods full of delightful walks.[4]

Stoneleigh's interior is a mixture of light, bright rooms with fine plasterwork and dark, timber panelled ones hung with family portraits in gilded frames from the time of the Lord Mayor, the original Thomas Leigh and founder of the family's fortunes, right up to the lunatic Edward, the last Lord Leigh. The abbey had its own chapel, wine and beer cellars, brew house, four and a half acres of kitchen gardens,

'As they drew near the end of their journey, her impatience for a sight of the Abbey...returned in full force, and every bend in the road was expected, with solemn awe to afford a glimpse of its massy walls of grey stone'
Northanger Abbey

a bakery, stables and cloisters all enclosed in quiet mature woodland with the river flowing through it. The mansion spoke of centuries of wealth, privilege and family continuity and its huge buildings and grounds a bulwark of might within the county and country. There is no doubt that Jane, Cassandra and her mother must have felt a little overawed and also proud of this connection. Although Jane Austen was very familiar with the large, modern and comfortable Kent houses of Goodnestone and Godmersham through her stays with her brother Edward, Stoneleigh Abbey outdid them both. First there were the ancient medieval buildings dating back to the twelfth century, lending mystery and interest, and then there was the ostentatious huge new west wing which spoke in obvious fashion of the wealth and importance of the family.

Mrs Austen noted the grandeur of the west wing:

45 windows in front, 15 in a row...the considerable flight of steps (some offices are under the house) into a large Hall: on the right hand the dining parlour, within that the

Breakfast room, where we generally sit, and reason good 'tis the only room (except the Chapel) that looks towards the River. On the left hand of the hall is the best drawing room, within that a smaller; these rooms are rather gloomy Brown wainscot and dark Crimson furniture; so we never use them but to walk thro' them to the old picture gallery. Behind the smaller drawing room is the state Bed Chamber, with a high crimson Velvet Bed: an alarming apartment just fit for a Heroine; the old gallery opens into it.[5]

The serpentine arrangement of the rooms and their unexpected juxtapositions are like Catherine Morland's experiences at Northanger Abbey when she goes in search of Mrs Tilney's bedroom fired by the belief that she will find some evidence of wrongdoing there, and on reaching it is disturbed by Henry Tilney at the top of stairs leading to the long gallery. At the time of Jane's visit to Stoneleigh the most direct route from the stables into the house, through the ground floor entrance, would bring you through a passageway to stairs that lead right up to the gallery just by 'the alarming apartment' – an arrangement that someone unfamiliar with the building would not expect.[6] Although *Northanger Abbey* was initially written around 1798 and first sold for publication in 1803 it was only published posthumously in 1818 having been retrieved from the publisher in 1816 who had done nothing with it, so it is feasible that Jane may have made some later revisions to the text.

With a housewife's eye Mrs Austen notes the exact number of bedrooms: '26 Bed Chambers in the new part of the house & a great many (some very good ones) in the old.' She even facetiously suggested to her cousin that signposts were needed for the guidance of his guests – 'I have proposed his setting up *directing Posts* at the Angles.'

How this all fits in with Fanny's tour of Sotherton in *Mansfield Park*:

The whole party rose accordingly, and under Mrs Rushworth's guidance were shewn through a number of rooms, all lofty, and many large and amply furnished in the taste of fifty years back, with shining floors, solid mahogany, rich damask, marble, gilding and carving, each handsome in its way.

Perhaps like the impressionable Fanny, Jane too listened to the stories about the family portraits at Stoneleigh with:

an unaffected earnestness to all that Mrs Rushworth could relate of the family in former times, its rise and grandeur, regal visits and loyal efforts, delighted to connect anything with history already known, or warm her imagination with scenes of the past.

There are paintings showing Jane Austen's great-grandfather, Theophilus Leigh with his mother-in-law, Lady Chandos; her son the first Duke of Chandos and his second wife, the Duchess Cassandra. There are two large portraits of nine of Theophilus'(I) and Mary Leigh's children, four in one painting and five in the other. The children are rather oddly painted with heads disproportionately large for their bodies, but Jane would not have minded as one of them showed her maternal grandfather, Thomas. No doubt her mother would have been overjoyed to see him portrayed as a child and pointed him and all her aunts and uncles out to her daughters. One portrait and its history in particular would have touched Jane's imagination – and she would already have heard of the lady in question at Adlestrop:

'The picture gallery, and two or three of the principal bedrooms, were all that remained to be shown...in the former were many good paintings'
Pride and Prejudice

Elizabeth Wentworth, the rich aunt and benefactress of the Adlestrop Leighs whose romantic story (see pages 34-35) and the name itself reappear in the story of Anne Elliot and her Captain Wentworth in *Persuasion*. The lady in question is portrayed fashionably dressed in fine creamy white satin with a prominent blue bow on the bodice of her opulent dress.

At Stoneleigh the party met every morning 'to say our prayers in a handsome chapel, the pulpit &c now being hung with Black.' This would have been the first instance of Jane either worshipping in or indeed seeing a private chapel at first hand. Like the chapel described at Sotherton, Stoneleigh's is:

> a mere, spacious oblong room fitted up for the purpose of devotion – with nothing more striking or more solemn than the profusion of mahogany, and the crimson velvet cushions appearing over the ledge of the family gallery above.[7]

Although Fanny finds this disappointing because of its lack of grandeur and sense of melancholy, the Georgian chapel at Stoneleigh with its large clear windows make it a light and airy space complemented by the simple beauty of the

'Having visited many more rooms than could be supposed to be of any other use than to contribute to the window tax, and find employment for housemaids, "Now" said Mrs Rushworth, "we are coming to the chapel..."'
Mansfield Park

white stucco plasterwork from the early eighteenth century. In 1763 Edward Leigh had commissioned William Gomm & Son, cabinet makers of Clerkenwell, to provide 150 new pieces of furniture for the house and the finest piece he made was the richly carved mahogany communion table for the chapel which Jane Austen must have noticed. The table fits well with the plasterwork and carvings which also feature the heads of cherubs – the bill for the table of £31.50 still survives.

Entry to the chapel gallery is from the first floor where one can look down onto the altar and nave by a bench where velvet cushions still remain – the same arrangement applies at Sotherton but Mrs Rushworth takes her visitors in on the ground floor as it is quicker. The chapel setting is cleverly used by Jane Austen for a vital twist in the plot as this is where Mary Crawford first learns 'to her horror' that Edmund is to be ordained[8].

While Mrs Austen was concerned with the lay-out and domestic arrangements within the Abbey what might an imaginative young woman make of it all? How she must have adored going around such a venerable house, gazing at the family portraits and taking a step back in time to conjure up her ancestors' past lives. She could also observe the even tempo of the great house, how its servants inside and out worked at providing every sort of food from fresh vegetables, bread, cheeses, butter and brewing beer for the household. A miniature model of the larger world steeped in tradition and a place where everyone knew their role in the scheme of things.

One of the other guests at Stoneleigh was the Reverend's niece the dowager Lady Saye & Sele, the mother-in-law of James Henry Leigh whose affected behaviour upset Mrs Austen but entertained Jane: 'Poor Lady Saye & Sele is rather tormenting, tho' sometimes amusing, and affords Jane many a good laugh – but she fatigues me sadly on the whole.'

Lady Saye & Sele questioned the clerk of the kitchen one evening to ask if 'the macaroni was made with Parmesan' and also said that since her husband's suicide she could not bear to eat chicken as 'after her lord destroyed himself she had eaten nicely boiled chicken for a fortnight in her chamber…and had not been able to eat it since'.

Lord Saye & Sele's notorious suicide was not an appropriate subject for a polite dinner party and probably bought the conversation to an embarrassing standstill. Perhaps Lady Saye

& Sele did know of Jane's novel writing (although none had been published at this time) because she also liked to talk about her sister, Cassandra Hawke, who had written a Gothic novel *Julia de Gramont* which Fanny Burney had dismissed as being about 'love, love, love, unmixed and unadulterated with any more worldly materials'. Before it was published in 1788 it had been in private circulation among the family so it is very possible that all the Austens had read it.

Fanny Burney had met both Lady Saye & Sele and Lady Hawke in 1782 and left us a vivid description of the pair:

> [Lady Saye & Sele] seems pretty near fifty—at least turned forty; her head was full of feathers, flowers, jewels, and gew-gaws... her dress trimmed with beads, silver, Persian sashes, and all sorts of fine fancies; her face is thin and fiery, and her whole manner spoke a lady all alive... Lady Hawke... is much younger than her sister , and rather pretty; extremely languishing, delicate and pathetic; apparently accustomed to be reckoned the genius of her family, and well contented to be looked upon as a creature dropped from the clouds.[9]

Like Mrs Norris who spent her time with the gardener and the housekeeper while the rest of the party walked in the grounds, Mrs Austen was fascinated by the cornucopia of resources the house offered in terms of food and drink:

> I do not fail to spend some time every day in the Kitchen Garden where the quantities of small fruits exceed anything you can form an idea of... The Garden contains 5 acres and a half. The ponds supply excellent Fish the Park excellent Venison; there is also great plenty of Pigeons, Rabbits & all sort of Poultry, a delightful Dairy where is made Butter good Warwickshire Cheese and Cream ditto. One Man Servant is called the Baker, He does nothing but Brew and

Bake. The quantity of Casks in the Strong Beer Cellar is beyond imagination: Those in the small Beer cellar bear no proportion, tho' by the bye the small Beer may be called Ale without misnomer.

For a woman who had, at Steventon grown and dug up her own potatoes, kept chickens and had to manage a large household almost single-handed, it must have seemed heaven indeed. The acquisitive Mrs Norris came away from her trip well satisfied with a gift of a 'beautiful little heath' from the gardener, and 'a cream cheese, just like the excellent one we had at dinner' from the housekeeper plus four beautiful pheasant eggs with which she planned to raise a brood with the help of her own hens. The Austens may have taken similar goodies to their Cooper cousins in Staffordshire. Mrs Austen was fond of her food, she wrote of their dinner on 13 August: 'And here we found ourselves on Tuesday…eating fish, venison, and all manner of good things, in a large and noble parlour hung around with family portraits.'[10] She spoke of breakfast which consisted of 'chocolate, coffee, and tea, plum cake, pound cake, hot rolls, cold rolls, bread and butter and dry toast for me'.[11]

In Bath the Austens had often been beholden for invitations to tea and suppers to eke out their own supplies as Jane had written to Cassandra in April of 1805:

We are engaged tomorrow Evening. What request we are in!– – Mrs Chamberlayne expressed to her neice her wish of being intimate enough with us to ask us to drink tea with her in a quiet way– We have therefore offered ourselves & our quietness thro' the same medium.– Our Tea and Sugar will last a great while.– I think we are just the kind of people & party to be treated about among our relations;–we cannot be supposed to be very rich.[12]

The abundance at Stoneleigh seemed a far cry from those days just over a year ago.

While Revd Thomas and Mr Hill were closeted over business every morning regarding legacies to servants at Stoneleigh and Grove House and continuing their correspondence with Leigh Perrot and his lawyers, Mrs Austen and her daughters

'...she viewed the respectable size and style of the building, its suitable, becoming, characteristic situation, low and sheltered – its ample gardens stretching down to meadows washed by a stream, of the Abbey, with all the old neglect of prospect, had scarcely a sight – and its abundance of timber in rows and avenues, which neither fashion nor extravagance had rooted up.'
Emma

enjoyed the grounds: '*We* walk a good deal, for the woods are impenetrable to the sun, even in the middle of an August day.'[13]

The beauty of trees and an abundance of timber are always admired in the novels and regarded as part and parcel of a good estate – and of course timber was an immensely valuable asset for a landowner and indeed at Stoneleigh this was part of its riches. Thornton Lacey's glebe meadows are 'finely sprinkled with timber', Pemberley has 'beautiful oaks and Spanish chestnuts' and Donwell Abbey 'an abundance of timber in rows and avenues, which neither fashion nor extravagance had rooted up'. The idea of cutting down the avenue of trees at Sotherton and Fanny's horror at the idea shows the revulsion felt at wanton destruction for the sake of the vanity of mere improvements. In *Sense and Sensibility* when Norland's old walnut trees are to be cut down to erect a greenhouse this is taken as yet another example of John Dashwood's lack of proper values.

In *Mansfield Park*, all the young people of the party also leave the glare of the sun on the terrace at Sotherton to walk in a wilderness, 'which was planted wood of about two acres, and though chiefly of larch and laurel, and beech cut down, and though laid out with too much regularity, was darkness and shade, and natural beauty...' At the end of the path are iron gates which lead onto more open ground and an oak grove on top of a knoll into which they all escape – apart from Fanny who is left alone on a bench looking over a ha-ha into the park. The impression of the expanse and size of the grounds all fit with the extensive parkland Jane would have seen at Stoneleigh.

Another member of the house party was a friend of James Henry Leigh, a distant relation called Robert Holt-Leigh described by Mrs Austen as 'the wrong side of forty; chatty and well-bred, and has a large estate'.

Robert Holt-Leigh was an MP for Wigan and was mentioned in a letter of Caroline Austen's to her niece, Emma Austen-Leigh:

> Aunt Cassandra told me, [that Mr Holt Leigh] was a great admirer...of her sister [Jane Austen]. They were all passing guests at Stoneleigh Abbey–& all passed away, & never met again...& I...mention this...only as showing that her pretty face did not pass through the world without receiving some tributes of admiration.[14]

Mr Holt-Leigh left Stoneleigh, but whether Jane regretted his loss we will never know; it is pleasant all the same to think that her self-confidence must have been boosted by his attentions. Replacing him at the Abbey was George Cooke, a cousin a little younger than herself of whom she was quite fond and had seen at Bath and written about, '...my Cousin George was very kind & talked sense to me every now & then in the intervals of his more animated fooleries with Miss Bendish, who is very young & rather handsome...'[15]

Then the Hon Mary Leigh's man of business, Joseph Hill, also left and, at last, Revd Thomas Leigh could turn his full attentions to his guests. It was no doubt a great joy to him to treat his relations to a series of sorties in the district which all had the extra dimension of a family connection to interest them. There was no difficulty in finding horses and carriages now. They went to Coombe Abbey, the seat of Lord Craven where Edward and the Hon. Mary Leigh may have stayed as children

'...they all returned to the house together, there to lounge away the time as they could with sofas, and chit-chat, and Quarterly Reviews, till the return of the others, and the arrival of dinner.'
Mansfield Park

after both their parents died leaving them minors. Their mother was Maria Craven, sister of Lord Craven who became a trustee for the young lord. Once a Cistercian abbey, Coombe had, like Stoneleigh, many buildings of the medieval era plus a new West Front that was added on in the 1680s – but much more successfully than Stoneleigh in terms of proportion and scale. Its grounds had been landscaped by Capability Brown and included an ornamental lake. (Today it is a luxury hotel). Once again Jane would have been reminded of the grandeur of her relations.

Grander still was Warwick Castle overlooking the River Avon – one of the most picturesque views in England. Again a tenuous family connection existed as Anne Whorwood married Ambrose Dudley, Earl of Warwick (brother to Queen Elizabeth's favourite, Robert Dudley). William Leigh I of Adlestrop, who died in 1632 married an Elizabeth Whorwood and their magnificent stone effigies rest in Gloucestershire at Longborough church. The romantic ruins of rosy-stoned Kenilworth Castle, slighted in the Civil War, was another favourite excursion.

The time at Stoneleigh must have flown by for Jane and left her with a multitude of impressions and memories. What a mixture Stoneleigh was – a Gothic abbey fused with modern opulence, extensive woods and winding paths, panelled chambers, long corridors, old stories and portraits, a tangled path to inheritance, eccentricities and madness – more than enough inspiration for any writer.

Late in August the Austens took their leave of the Revd Thomas and his sister and continued their way to the more mundane destination of the parsonage at Hamstall Ridware in Staffordshire.

CHAPTER NINE

The Reverend Leigh at the Abbey

'Sotherton Court is the noblest old place in the world.'
Mansfield Park

It is time now to describe the estate and lands at Stoneleigh in Warwickshire – Shakespeare's county – which Jane, her mother and sister journeyed to in the late summer of 1806. Stoneleigh's old name was Stoneleigh-in-Arden, a place once on the fringes of the ancient forest, and although much of the woodland had been cleared, there were still many venerable trees in the park and, as mentioned, part of the value of the estate was in its timber.

Stoneleigh Abbey is an extraordinary collection of buildings spanning many centuries. The medieval gatehouse, the north and south wings are constructed from building materials cannibalised from the original Cistercian abbey, which blends into the landscape. Their Gothic frontages and windows are surrounded by the rosy pink Kenilworth stone of the area in a harmonious style, they are pleasant and attractive, whereas the huge west wing of grey stone seems to loom quite startlingly out of proportion and style in comparison to the earlier structure. This enormous edifice was built in 1720 by Francis Smith, a master-builder in the Midlands, under the direction of the third Lord Leigh, Edward, the grandfather of the 'lunatic lord'. In Pevsner it is described as 'the grandest, most dramatic Georgian mansion of Warwickshire.'

'...Northanger Abbey having been a richly endowed convent at the time of the Reformation, of its having fallen into the hands of an ancestor of the Tilneys on its dissolution, of a large portion of its ancient building still making a part of the present dwelling...'
Northanger Abbey

Inside the west wing, the finest room is the saloon, with stucco medallions that take the classical legend of Hercules as their subject matter. It is a masterpiece of baroque carving in exquisite plasterwork probably by the hands of Italian artisans. This great space and other modernising improvements to the house were all, as already mentioned in Chapter Two, accomplished during the fifth Lord Leigh's time before his illness overtook him, but little was undertaken to alter the grounds or gardens to enhance the magnificence of the new wing.

The Revd Thomas Leigh had known Stoneleigh since he was a boy having paid visits to his cousins throughout his life but it is intriguing to imagine how, aged seventy-two, he would have felt taking on this vast legacy so different in scale and importance to his village parsonage. One thing he was keenly aware of was the lack of a view or picturesque aspect. Instead of the quiet green lawns and cricket ground which the frontage now overlooks, there was a nondescript farm and a motley collection of assorted buildings. The river, which runs close to the sloping lawns by the side of the house, was then a little further away across farmland and woods. Would he have been delighted to imagine himself lord of this? Or daunted? No matter, he was a man of principle, and saw himself as a caretaker for his nephew; by grasping the nettle of the inheritance and thrashing out a deal with contenders like Leigh Perrot he ensured a golden future for the Leighs of Adlestrop.

One of Julia Leigh's friends who visited the house in 1810, named Maria Berry, disliked the west wing calling it:

one of the worst-contrived large houses of fourteen windows in front that I ever saw…the present possessors, an old clergyman and his sister are perfectly encumbered with the wealth, to which they succeeded in a late period of life, and which obliged them to leave a comfortable parsonage, where they had passed their best years.[1]

A point of view echoed by Caroline Austen who wrote in 1867, 'the change came too late in their lives to be pleasant to them.'[2] Agnes Leigh writing her 1910 *Memoir* continues the theme, 'He [the Reverend Thomas Leigh] presently made arrangements with the head of the family James Henry Leigh who took possession of Stoneleigh and Thomas returned to his peaceful existence in Adlestrop!'[3]

Caroline elaborated on how Thomas and Elizabeth managed their affairs: 'He retained his living that he and his sister might still spend some part of the year in the old home they loved so well…of course Mr Leigh provided a curate…' In 1806 a letter from one of Stoneleigh's servants to Joseph Hill felt it was all too much for the old pair and certainly for Elizabeth Leigh: 'Mrs E Leigh has been very unwell I think two much bustale [sic] for her.'[4]

'The house was built in Elizabeth's time, and is a large, regular brick building — heavy but respectable looking, and has many good rooms. It stands in one of the lowest spots of the park; in that respect unfavourable for improvement. But the woods are fine, and there is a stream…'
Mansfield Park

As a young girl Caroline visited Stoneleigh with her parents, James and Mary Austen in 1809 and remembers all the outings her father undertook to nearby attractions just like Jane had done three years earlier:

…excursions were made most days to see something

– Warwick Castle, Guys Cliff, Combe Abbey and Kenilworth…one day he went to Warwick Races with a party from the house. Mr Leigh was not among them and a Visitors Carriage was used, for he would not suffer his own to appear on the course, deeming it improper that a Clergman's equipage should be seen there…[5]

After the careful stewardship of the Revd Thomas Leigh and James Henry the Stoneleigh properties in the mid to late nineteenth century produced an annual income in excess of £30,000, a figure worth well over a million pounds today – compare this with the richest of all Jane Austen's characters, Mr Rushworth, whose income was £12,000 a year. The Leigh family remained the largest landholders in Warwickshire in Victorian England: an 1883 survey calculated their landholdings at 14,891 acres. In 1946 Stoneleigh Abbey was one of the first stately homes to be opened to the public and over 36,000 visitors came to view it before a terrible fire in 1960 which badly damaged the west wing. Luckily much of the furniture, artworks and the plasterwork in the saloon were saved with the help of Lord Leigh and the people on the estate but the house had to close. It took many years and much work and fundraising via the Stoneleigh Abbey Preservation Trust before it was reopened to the public in 1984. In 1996 the fifth Lord Leigh (of the second creation) transferred all the property to the Stoneleigh Abbey Preservation Trust and was one of their trustees. Now the estate is run by a board of trustees and the Leighs no longer play any part in its development – the head of the family has returned to live and farm in Adlestrop. One interesting anomaly remains – in the parkland many of the trees still belong to the family

'The park was very large, and contained great variety of ground. They entered it at one of its lowest points, and drove for some time through a beautiful wood…'
Pride and Prejudice

and if they need pruning or felling the Trust has to apply to them for permission. The house has now been magnificently refurbished inside and the Trust is currently working with Natural England to restore the bridges including the iron bridge, the weirs and sluices so they can bring Repton's vision back to life and create walks around the parkland for visitors.

In the village of Stoneleigh itself the red sandstone church of St Mary with its splendid zigzag arches dating from the Norman period are full of Leigh memorials. Perhaps the most poignant is the plainest of them all – tucked away in the upper right hand wall of the chancel – to 'The Right Honourable Edward Lord Leigh born 1st of March 1742/3 Died 26 May 1786.'

Nearby, but considerably more prominent, is the tablet to his sister, Mary Leigh described as 'sole heiress of Edward, the fifth Lord Leigh having survived her brother 20 years.' Away from the church in a quiet far corner of the churchyard the fifth Lord Leigh of the second creation, John Piers Leigh has a small stone recording only his dates of birth and death: 1935-2003. His funeral was a lively affair, packed with people and the accompaniment of a jazz band.

It was of course, the Revd Thomas Leigh, who after his experiences in Adlestrop with the great improvements to the grounds of his parsonage and the park, employed Humphry Repton in 1808 to work his magic at Stoneleigh. Instead of the paltry acreage at Adlestrop, the Stoneleigh gardens and 320-acre deer park were surrounded by a thousand acres and had the wonderful advantage of the River Avon running near the house. One of the treasures held at Stoneleigh is the Red Book that Humphry Repton prepared which shows his ideas for improving the house and grounds. Although it appears to have been rebound at some stage its contents are in immaculate condition with exquisite pen and ink and colour drawings featuring 'before and after' flaps of views plus a clear map. It was lost for a while but thankfully found behind some other volumes in a bookcase. The text, written in brown ink, is beautifully clear.

The book is addressed to Thomas Leigh by Repton on the opening page and was delivered in May 1809. It is one of the few extant large format Red Books given to other important clients such as the Prince Regent at the Brighton Pavilion and the Duke of Bedford at Woburn Abbey. It must have been an object of great wonderment and delight to open its thick cream pages.

Repton was famous for his obsequious manner to his patrons and this is borne out here:

> In my endeavours to elucidate this interesting subject I must continually regret the inability of my pencil to describe what I feel – while I derive some satisfaction from the consideration, that I am addressing myself to you: who have displayed so much good taste in what has been done at Adlestrop under your own immediate direction, and who have been pleased occasionally to consult me on that subject...I must therefore congratulate you on having this more ample field to display your taste – at the same time that I congratulate the country, on this most ancient home (so long preserved in the same family) – having now a possessor who knows both how to value, and how to improve its Natural Beauties.

It was not a straightforward task for Repton; he referred to Stoneleigh as 'an object of great magnitude...it represents circumstances very different from any other place in which I have ever been consulted'.[6] The Stoneleigh Red Book is as unique as Repton found the subject because, unlike any others that survive, he illustrated his ideas for the house and gardens with a series of delicate watercolours which aped, in turn, great masters such as Claude Lorrain, Watteau and Ruysdael because these artists had the ability to blend age 'with graceful forms and antiquity combined with elegance'. Repton noted the huge differences in architectural styles at Stoneleigh which included the medieval gatehouse, the Gothic charms of its North Front, the narrowness of the South Front, and the rich style of the West Elevation reflecting that,

> the buildings at Stoneleigh present curious specimens of architecture of every date, from the 10th to the 18th century...The changes in the taste of the nation are as little directed by reason, as that of individuals – there are certain objects which please or displease certain persons at certain times, without any apparent cause.

He admitted the lack of unity between the new palace and the old gateway but was firmly of the opinion that 'although these two may not class together in point of date, they both belong to the same class as objects of beauty...that is, they are both picturesque'. Repton was a practical man and determined to make the best of what he found and also he did not believe in destroying buildings even when they were not in the current fashion – something for which we can thank him. He made sensible suggestions for a new servants' entrance and access for carts and horses and for improving the approach to the Abbey by building a bridge to the west to 'shorten the distance to Warwick, to Coventry, to Kenilworth, to the village, and to the Park'. He laments the narrow frontage of the South Front which is out of proportion to the West having only four windows and suggests an ambitious plan of adding three windows and 'addition of sculpture and vases and ballustraded terraces' which he feels 'would present a scene of beauty far beyond my pencil's power to express'.

Repton's thoughts on the west wing of the Abbey are

revealing, calling it 'a great Pile' which inside was 'not conformable to the present manner of living, which consists of large rooms arranged *en suite*…with the best apartments looking to the best view'. He considered that the new rooms on the first floor although of a good size were 'oppressed by the comparative great size of the Hall, which separates instead of connecting the two ends of the house'. He had many ideas on how to improve the house, to soften its exterior, for instance with a series of colonnaded terraces on the southwest but none of these plans were carried out. On the 'before' picture of the side of the West Front he shows how the view is totally obscured by a long stone wall which enclosed a bowling green in front of the house. Just like Henry Crawford who, when looking for places open to improvement at Sotherton, also pounced on the old-fashioned bowling green and longed to dismantle its walls:

> Mr Crawford was the first to move forward, to examine the capabilities of that end of the house. The lawn, bounded on each side by a high wall, contained beyond the first planted area, a bowling green…it was a good spot for fault-finding.[7]

Even before the completion of the Red Book, the Revd Leigh was keen to start changes to the forecourt of the west front and the river frontage on the south side of the house. The work on the river was crucial to Repton's vision about 'The Water'. He had three aims:

> 1st: To produce a larger surface of water in view of the Abbey
> 2nd To account for the increased breadth by showing it to be the conflux of two different streams
> 3rd To add to this intricacy by a channel of water falling from a higher level and by contrasting the effects of foam and water in rapid motion – with the calm of a glassy

surface – and lastly to make such walks and pleasure grounds on the banks of the water as may show all its interesting features to advantage.

His idea here was much the same as the work he had carried out at Adlestrop albeit on a much smaller scale. Indeed in one of his sketches he remarks:

> The models for some other of my sketches have been taken from the imaginary scenes of Claude, Watteau and Ruysdale; but this is taken from real scenes at Adlestrop, where the water is shown thro openings, most judiciously preserved, between groups of larger trees in the foreground.... I have only to recommend the same good taste and management, which has succeeded so well at Adlestrop, to produce still greater effects at Stoneleigh Abbey.

This is the famous 'View' still visible today from the Grove which Repton engineered by clearing a knoll of undergrowth and giving a vantage point over the calm lake waters to the house rising in the distance. Whether the trees in the foreground were painted from his memory of the lakes at Adlestrop it is now impossible to tell as they are all so overgrown. In my opinion the idea may have sprung from the view of the parsonage from the 'Little Lakes' rather than one from the larger lake at the bottom of the meadow.

One of his Watteau-style watercolours has a 'before' picture of the riverside frontage with a man – possibly Repton himself – supervising some workmen in pegging out a line with stakes showing changes to the course of the River Avon. Repton explains why he chose Watteau as his inspiration for this scene:

> ...without the slightest attempt to make one of his pictures my model — but the richness, the amenity and

the cheerfulness of his scenery, have made a very accurate dilettanti observe that as the figures of Rembrandt, tho' crouded with Jewells and Embroidery, always present dirty old Men and Women — so the pictures of Watteau amidst Shepherds and Gardeners seem to introduce us to elegant Society.[8]

Many of Repton's ideas were not carried through but his ideas on the river were. Just as in the 'after' drawings, the course of the flow was changed to generate a reflective pool in front of the house and the joining of two streams made for a lively contrast to this stillness. A new approach road to the Abbey from the west was another of Repton's ideas but it was finally constructed not to his exact direction, but over a straighter course. A new stone bridge was erected and John Rennie started on this in 1812. Of course when Jane and her family came to Stoneleigh in 1806 none of this would have been in evidence because the work did not begin until 1809, at the earliest, but she had already seen Repton's influence at first hand in Adlestrop and perhaps was informed of the changes through Elizabeth Leigh's letters to the family. Other Austens visited Stoneleigh too and would have reported their impressions and their news back to Jane and her mother.

'...but the gate was locked. Mr Rushworth wished he had bought the key; he had been very near thinking whether he should not bring the key; he was determined he would never come without the key again; but still this did not remove the present evil.'
Mansfield Park

Miss Berry was able to see Mr Repton at work in the grounds together with Mrs Leigh and the Revd Thomas Leigh:

We passed the house or abbey...and drove on to the park. Before we entered we met our acquaintance Mrs Leigh (whose husband is to succeed to the place after the present incumbent), and the old incumbent himself, and Mr Repton planning future improvements; very probably, like the Irishman's, for the worse. They gave us a key to the park, but we continued on foot, and were lead by Greathead to the most beautiful parts of the most beautiful woodland scenery…if this park shows marks of neglect, it is, at least unspoiled by improvement.[9]

Miss Berry was almost echoing the thought of Fanny Price herself on the folly of improvements. We should remember that the suggestion of employing Repton at Sotherton was made by Maria Bertram who is later revealed as an amoral adultress and afforded no forgiveness by her creator. Mary Berry's description is a tantalising reminder of one of the crucial scenes at Sotherton in *Mansfield Park* – the giving of a key to open the iron gates to allow exploration of the parkland.

Mary Berry also experienced a sycophantic display from the great improver himself: 'We met Mrs Leigh and her party on our road home. Mr Repton (whom I had never seen before) fired off an exceeding fine complimentary speech to Agnes and me from the window of the carriage.'[10]

The death of Revd Leigh in 1813 was to mean an end to Repton's work on Stoneleigh. James Henry Leigh did not continue to employ him and paid off his outstanding account of fifty guineas (only ten days' work according to Jane Austen's reckoning) on 26 October 1813.[11] Although Repton was no longer personally involved, much of the future work on the grounds bear the hallmarks of his inspirational style. Over the next decade new parkland was increased to a thousand acres around the Abbey and the deer park was improved which all resulted in a landscape that Repton and doubtless the Revd Leigh would both have approved of.

The Adlestrop Leighs from this time on now made Stoneleigh their main residence visiting Adlestrop only occasionally, but kept in close touch through their agents as to what was happening in the village. One regular posting to a descendant was about each season's hunting: 'Your Lordship will be glad to know that Adlestrop continues to be as famous as ever for its breed of foxes: we have had so many this year that hounds had killed nine before the frost set in and there are as yet a great many more.'

James Henry Leigh with his stalwart wife, Julia spent a small fortune of some £13,000 in a ten year period on furniture, pictures, china, plate, chandeliers, carpets, wallpapers plus 82 yards of crimson velvet for furniture covers and curtains. The house's structure was hardly changed but a new stable block and riding house were built.[12]

The Leighs whom Jane Austen knew personally gradually disappeared from the scene: James Henry in 1823 and Julia twenty years later in 1843. Both are commemorated in Adlestrop church in an elegant marble memorial tablet on the wall of the South Aisle with a Grecian urn and the Leigh arms above it with the legend: *James Henry Leigh Esquire d. October 28 1823 aged 58 years and his relict Julia Judith Leigh (daughter of Thomas 10th Lord Saye and Sele) who is interred in the vault at Stoneleigh.*

Their son and heir, Chandos Leigh (1791-1850), hardly dabbled in improvements although in the late 1840s he used the garden designer, W.A. Nesfield, to advise him on both Stoneleigh and Adlestrop. The crowning achievement for the splendid estate that Stoneleigh had become was the visit by Queen Victoria and Prince Albert on 14-16 June 1858. The pretty rooms at the side of the house so enjoyed by the Austens for breakfasting in, became the royal couple's suite where they could gaze at the river gliding by. Queen Victoria planted an oak in the grounds and Prince Albert a *Wellingtonia gigantia*.[13]

One further twist in the family fortunes would have been

welcomed by Jane Austen and all the Adlestrop Leighs: in 1839 Chandos Leigh was created the first Baron Leigh of the second creation by the Prime Minister, Lord Melbourne. Julia had fought for this for many years but the case had been bedevilled by a false pretender, a George Leigh from Lancashire who had claimed descent from the first Lord Leigh. Eventually his claims were shown to have no foundation and the peerage was restored to the Leigh family and Queen Victoria was pleased to dub him Baron Leigh of Stoneleigh.[14]

When Chandos died abroad in 1850 his widow moved to Adlestrop with the youngest of her children and died in 1860. The son and heir, the second baron, Lord William Henry Leigh, was secure in the knowledge that he would inherit Stoneleigh and this pattern was unbroken for the next hundred years. During his tenure of Stoneleigh William Leigh was to experience a downfall in his income caused by reduced rents; its income slipped to £23,000 annually, hardly more than when the Revd Thomas Leigh inherited Stoneleigh in 1806, although the cost of living had gone up tremendously. On his death in 1905 the heady times for Stoneleigh began to decline, ultimately leading to the transfer of the estate to a trust in 1979. Although the Leighs were forced in the twentieth century to sell much of their land to meet heavy death duties and increased taxation they never gave up Adlestrop and today the village is the home of Lord Christopher Leigh, the sixth baron of the second creation.

CHAPTER TEN

A Bevy of Vicars: Clerical Connections

'Her father was a clergyman, without being neglected or poor, and a very respectable man, though his name was Richard, and he had never been handsome. He had a considerable independence, besides two good livings and he was not in the least addicted to locking up his daughters.'
Northanger Abbey

Jane Austen was certainly surrounded by clergymen – her maternal grandfather, father, two of her brothers and four of her cousins were all ordained. And of course her host at Adlestrop, Thomas Leigh was the rector.

The clergy play a prominent role in her novels including among others the deliciously sanctimonious Mr Collins in *Pride and Prejudice*, the indolent and epicurean Dr Grant in *Mansfield Park*, Henry Tilney in *Northanger Abbey* and the 'very handsome' Mr Elton in *Emma*. Edward Ferrers in *Sense and Sensibility* is offered a lifeline by Colonel Brandon who endows him a living in his gift thereby allowing Edward to marry his true love, Elinor Dashwood. A few curates such as Charles Hayter and Mr Wentworth in *Persuasion* are often mentioned as part of the country scene.

Much of the plot of *Mansfield Park* hinges on Edmund Bertram's decision to become a clergyman and indeed some authorities believe Jane Austen herself said in a letter composed when she was halfway through the writing of the novel[1] that the subject of the book was 'ordination'.[2] This is disputed by a recent biographer, Park Honan, who thinks this letter has been wrongly transcribed and the word in question does not refer to *Mansfield Park* at all but merely refers to an enquiry Cassandra had answered about 'clerical ordination at James's rectory'.[3]

It is tempting to wonder how much Jane Austen drew from life in her characterisations when she had such a large number of clergy known to her at first hand to draw upon. It is also noteworthy that she felt no particular need to be respectful to the profession but was quite content to highlight their comical or unattractive aspects; she was well aware that the Church and its officers were not universally popular or respected despite the belief of Mr Collins to the contrary: '...give me leave to observe that I consider the clerical office as equal in point of dignity with the highest rank in the kingdom...'

The fictional incumbent who most resembles the Revd Thomas Leigh might be Dr Grant simply because he is middle-aged, childless and married – however we have no record that Thomas Leigh was a gourmand and he was certainly not as lazy as Dr Grant appears to be. Much mocked by Mary Crawford he is accused of pretending illness when faced with a tough dish of pheasant and quarrelling with his wife over 'a green goose, which he could not get the better of'. Stronger opprobrium is voiced by her too: '...though Dr Grant is most kind and obliging to me, and though he is really a gentleman, and I dare say a good scholar and clever, and often preaches good sermons, and is very respectable, I see him to be an indolent selfish bon vivant.' Fanny Price, always looking to say the right thing, tries to stick up for the doctor and believes that he will become a better person because he preaches such good sermons. Dr Grant actually dies from greed when he is able to leave Mansfield and move 'through an interest on which he had almost ceased to form hopes to a stall in Westminster' and then 'brought on apoplexy and death by three great institutionary dinners in one week.'

The clergy were always a lynchpin in any village and from her childhood Jane was aware of their duties to poor parishioners. As a rector's daughter she, like Emma Woodhouse, must have visited the poor in their cottages and urged them to come with their pitchers to fetch broth from the Austen's kitchen. (A practice bitterly remembered by Mrs Norris when it was impossible to know, 'how much was consumed in our kitchen by odd comers and goers'.) In a neat juxtaposition, Emma who has just come from a visit to a destitute family in Highbury, by chance meets Mr Elton and though he is interested to hear of all the 'wants and sufferings of the poor family' then relates his own tale of a party at his friends the day before, listing 'the Stilton cheese, the north Wiltshire, the butter, the celery, the beet-root and all the dessert.'

'She liked him the better for being a clergyman, "for she must confess herself very partial to the profession", and something like a sigh escaped her as she said it.'
Northanger Abbey

There is much discussion in all of the novels about the likelihood of 'livings' coming up and how much they are worth and it is obvious that these were matters that Jane Austen knew about and took a close interest in. She was aware of all the controversies over pluralism and absentee incumbents, the poverty of curates, the sellings of livings and the dangers of simony. Today we tend to imagine that the clergy choose their profession because of a personal vocation and because they have a strong Christian faith but in the eighteenth and nineteenth centuries more pragmatic views were adopted. Socially it seems to have been taken for granted that everyone shared a belief in the teaching of the Church and in the value of its place in the community.

Edward Ferrers puts the case for entering the Church succinctly:

It has been, and is, and probably always will be a heavy misfortune to me, that I have had no necessary business to engage me, no profession to give me employment, or afford me anything like independence. But unfortunately my own nicety, and the nicety of my friends, have made me what I am, an idle helpless being. We could never agree in my choice of a profession. I always preferred the church, as I still do. But that was not smart enough for my family.

The younger sons of the gentry and the aristocracy such as the real Thomas Leigh and the fictional Edmund Bertram were prime candidates to enter the profession and their appointment was always down to patronage or nepotism.

Patronage at least implied that the landowners actively looked for clergymen whom they believed would help their communities and this is something that Jane Austen felt had a very useful role in underpinning rural life. Her ideal parish was, like Adlestrop, a place where the manor house, the church and the parsonage were all 'within a stone's throw' of each other just like Delaford in *Sense and Sensibility*. Part of the attraction of being a member of the clergy was that even though the incumbent might be relatively poor compared to their richer neighbours, they would still be considered as part of the same 'class' to be included in the social round, that is they would always be thought of as gentlemen.

'It is fortunate that your inclination and your father's convenience should accord so well. There is a very good living kept for you, I understand, hereabouts.'
Mansfield Park

Apart from currying favour how exactly did the system of patronage and granting livings work?

The initial qualification for being ordained was to study for a degree from either Oxford or Cambridge – the only two universities in existence in England at the time. At the end of the eighteenth century about sixty per cent of graduates entered the church.[4] The first hurdle was to have the means to enter one of these exclusive colleges. For the poor it was virtually impossible, grammar schools had declined and it was necessary to have a sound base of classical learning for admission and later success. The availability of scholarships was quite limited although public schools and some of the richer grammar schools had several in their gift.

> 'How proper Mr.Tilney might be as a dreamer or a lover, had not yet, perhaps entered Mr Allen's head, but that he... had been assured of Mr.Tilney's being a clergyman, and of a very respectable family in Gloucestershire.'
> *Northanger Abbey*

Jane's father, George Austen had had an extraordinarily lucky upbringing which enabled him to gain a scholarship to St John's College, Oxford.

George's parents had both died when he was a child and it was due to the kindness of his uncle Francis Austen, a successful solicitor and landowner, that he attended the grammar school at Tonbridge and from there obtained his scholarship. Once at Oxford he would have mixed with all the other undergraduates, many of them sons of peers and landowners and hopefully made many useful contacts. Mr Collins is looked down on in *Pride and Prejudice* because 'though he belonged to one of the universities, he had merely kept the necessary terms, without forming any useful acquaintance.'

Clergy were often seen as figures of fun – when Robert Ferrars hears that his brother is about to accept a living:

He laughed most immoderately. The idea of Edward's being a clergyman, and living in a small parsonage-house diverted him beyond measure; and when to that was added the fanciful imagery of Edward reading prayers in a white surplice...he could conceive of nothing more ridiculous.

At Oxford University the BA course of four years (often reduced to three) concentrated mainly on the classics with about a third of its syllabus on the 'sciences': logic, rhetoric, Euclid, morals and politics. There was no special theology course even for those destined for the cloth. The final examinations were oral and failure was rare. Once given a degree, a candidate for ordination needed a testimonial from his college that would show he was suitable – again a formality – and then a bishop had to be found to ordain him. This was meant to be a test of the candidate's knowledge of scripture, Latin, the liturgy and the Thirty-Nine Articles but their standards were lax and few were ever refused. Henry Austen mugged up the Greek Testament when he applied for ordination some twenty years after his graduation but the bishop did not bother him on the topic.[5]

Taking Orders was not allowed until the candidate had reached the age of twenty-three and therefore many graduates were left kicking their heels after finishing university. The solution for George Austen was to take up a university fellowship with an annual value of about a hundred pounds which could be renewed year on year and to take on clerical duties in villages within a short ride's distance. Marrying meant an end to a fellowship and intensified the desire for a parish that would pay a comfortable sum to its incumbent and also include a decent family home.

> 'What! Take orders without a living! No, that is madness indeed, absolute madness!'
> *Mansfield Park*

Comfortable livings were in short supply towards the end of the eighteenth century when the number of clergy had multiplied making it an overcrowded profession. Many waiting for a living to come up would put themselves up for hire – taking services where the incumbent was an absentee and where there was no curate. These young men were known as 'gallopers' and they would ride around the countryside, either from their colleges, or from rented rooms in country towns, performing as many services as they could pack in on a Sunday.

Even curacies were hard to come by and without any security or certainty that they would lead to better things. An appointment was made when either the resident vicar was unwilling to undertake all the duties that his parish warranted and needed a curate to fulfil many of his obligations, or where there was an absentee incumbent and the curate acted in his place. In both instances it was up to the individual vicar to pay the curate from his own pocket and naturally they tried to pay as little as they could. Acts of Parliament and decrees from the bishops tried to fix a decent income for curates but they were ineffective and the average yearly income of curates in the 1790s was a meagre £35.

> 'Wait for his having a living — aye, we all know how that will end; they will wait a twelvemonth, and finding no good comes of it, will set down upon a curacy of fifty pounds a-year…then they will have a child every year! And Lord help 'em! How poor they will be.'
> *Sense and Sensibility*

Another practice was that of keeping a living 'warm' for a future incumbent who was not yet old enough to take it up or perhaps had not yet been ordained. This is how Charles Hayter in *Persuasion*, 'nothing but a country curate' is able to marry Henrietta. His prospects were made better by the fact that the parish was 'in the centre of some of the best preserves in the kingdom, surrounded by three great proprietors… and to two of the three at least, Charles Hayter might get a special recommendation'. Although his brother-in-law to be, Charles Musgrove, worries that Hayter's lack of enthusiasm for 'sporting' – i.e. shooting, might let him down. Many clergymen were famous for their hunting exploits which would always make them popular in a rural environment.

Jane's elder brother, James, was one such who took great pleasure in the thrill of the chase. While he was at Oxford he was the author of a spoof publication called *The Loiterer* in which he encouraged country parsons to have 'an extensive and accurate knowledge of all sporting matters…for nothing is more certain than a good shot has brought down a comfortable Vicarage, and many a bold rider lept into a snug Rectory.'[6]

In her letters Jane is always wishing good sport for her brothers when they came back to Steventon. Fox hunting with a pack of hounds became popular in the mid-eighteenth century, before then deer had been the main quarry. Hunting with hounds and shooting game birds needed permission from the lord of the manor. Jane's father shared the lordship of Steventon manor with the tenant of the manor house, Hugh Digweed, by courtesy of the family's great benefactor, Thomas Knight. Coincidentally Adlestrop was a place remarked upon for its excellent fox hunting and pheasant shooting and, even today, Adlestrop pheasant is singled out on local restaurant menus in Cotswold gastro pubs and hunting (with a scent) carries on, with the hunt meeting sometimes at Adlestrop before flying across the fields with their hounds leading the way.

Hunting was essential to stave off the boredom often felt by young men during the long country winters in isolated villages. By necessity most middle class families kept horses for transport and though the young men might not have been so well mounted as their aristocratic neighbours they could still perform well. Francis Austen, Jane's favourite elder brother, had a pony which he purchased for £1 11s 6d at the age of only seven which he rode to hounds for a couple of years before selling it on at a small profit.

The Austen sons were able to gain entry to Oxford University because of their maternal grandmother, Jane Walker, née Perrot. The Perrots were 'kin' to the founder of St John's College, Oxford, Sir Thomas White and all the cousins of this large family could claim admission on this slender connection.[7] This was the route that Jane's brothers James and Henry took to be admitted to St John's.

Naturally none of this could help the two Austen sisters as women were not admitted to either university and a career in the Church was also completely out of bounds to them – the chance of further education for women in England would happen in 1869 – while the Anglican Church waited until the late twentieth century to allow female ordination.

At the end of the eighteenth century there were about 11,600 benefices in England and Wales and the way to find one varied. About six hundred were in the gift of the public schools and the two universities of Oxford and Cambridge – often designed for Masters and Fellows who wished to exchange a life of celibacy for marriage. The rich pickings belonged to bishops and cathedral chapters who accounted for about 2,500 livings – it was possibly one of these that Dr Grant gained when he moved to Westminster from Mansfield. If you had a relation connected to a bishop you stood a fighting chance of preferment. About a thousand livings were held by the Crown but here again you needed personal connections to the high and mighty to obtain one. But the majority of the 5,500 odd livings were in the hands of private landowners and this is the most common circumstance that Jane Austen's relations and her characters would find themselves in.[8] The Austens were well connected on every side including the Leigh links whereby James Austen had the two livings of Cubbington and Hunningham courtesy of the Hon. Mary Leigh and Edward Cooper took the living at Hamstall Ridware by the same route. Jane's father, first via a cousin, 'inherited' the living of

'I have been so fortunate as to be distinguished by the patronage of the Right Honourable Lady Catherine de Bourgh...whose bounty and beneficence has preferred me to the valuable rectory of this parish...'
Pride and Prejudice

Steventon which was in the gift of Edward's benefactor, Thomas Knight and then had the living at nearby Deane bought for him by his generous uncle Francis. The Revd Leigh took over the living at Adlestrop following in his uncle's footsteps which was in the gift of his brother, James Leigh.

The clergy were certainly ubiquitous in society as William Cobbett observed in 1802:

> The clergy are less powerful from their rank and industry than from their *locality*. They are from necessity *everywhere*, and their aggregate influence is astonishingly great…it is in the equal distribution of the clergy, their being in every corner of the country which makes them such a formidable corps.[9]

George Austen was no doubt hastened into retirement from his parish of Steventon when his own son, James, in 1794 was promised the living on its next presentation and then moved with his young family into the nearby village of Deane as curate. Knowing how small their house was and how little money James would have, their proximity must have had a bearing on George and his wife's sudden decision to retire to Bath in 1800. Jane herself was taken aback when she learnt of it and apparently fainted when she heard the news. Later in a letter to Cassandra she writes rather bitterly:

'…a country curate, without bread to eat.'
Persuasion

> My father's old Ministers are already deserting him to pay their court to his Son; the brown Mare, which as well as the black was to devolve on James at our removal, has not had patience to wait for that, & has settled herself even now at Deane.[10]

It was ironic that George Austen himself had obtained his second living in a similar fashion thanks to his Uncle Francis buying the next presentation for Deane & Ashe in 1770. Deane fell vacant first and became the Austens' first home. Francis Austen then sold Ashe on to Benjamin Langlois who, in his turn, could help his nephew George Lefroy to a living. None of this nepotism or favouritism shocked Jane Austen but she drew the line at the practice of a landowner who had an advowson, offering it for sale in a newspaper advertisement which listed the value of the living and the life expectancy of its present holder and invited bids. In *Sense and Sensibility* she highlights the poor ethics of John Dashwood by showing his astonishment on hearing the news that Colonel Brandon has *given* the living of Delaford to Edward Ferrars, instead of selling it when he might have accrued a handsome profit of £1400: 'I wonder he should be so improvident in a point of such common, such natural concern!'

In contrast Sir Thomas Bertram was deeply regretful that he had been forced to sell the living at Mansfield Park to meet the gambling debts of Edmund's elder brother, Tom. This was why 'the presentation became the right of Dr Grant'. Luckily the living at Thornton Lacey was still reserved for Edmund and in *Mansfield Park* an interesting discussion takes place between Edmund Bertram, destined for Ordination, the heroine Fanny Price and the skittish Mary Crawford on the desirability of becoming a member of the clergy. Mary questions Edmund's motives by inferring he only wishes for this because he knows he will have a good living – a charge vigorously refuted by both him and Fanny. In Mary's jaundiced view '...a clergyman has nothing to do but to be slovenly and selfish – read the newspaper, watch the weather and quarrel with his wife. His curate does all the work, and the business of his own life is to dine.'

Edmund appears to have a real vocation but he, and Edward Ferrers are almost alone in considering religious belief as a calling among Jane Austen's depictions of the clergy. In a reaction to the general complacency about religion the Evangelical movement or 'Christian Revival' began in the 1730s. The early proponents of the movement such as George Whitefield were from a poor background and the only way they could study at Oxford was to act as a 'servitor' in exchange for free tuition. This meant that they worked for more prosperous undergraduates – waking them up in the morning, performing menial tasks such as polishing their shoes, and even, in some cases writing their essays for them.

'For what is to be done in the church? Men love to distinguish themselves, and in either of the other lines, distinction may be gained, but not in the church. A clergyman is nothing.'
Mansfield Park

In Adlestrop the living had always been in the gift of the Leigh family. Originally the village church was annexed to Broadwell in the Stow Deanery and therefore the rector officiated at both villages. Centuries passed before late in the seventeenth century the vicar, Richard Johnson, built or restored the glebe house of '6 bays and 8 hearths' in Adlestrop and came to live there and the glebe house and lands in Broadwell were let. In Sir Robert Atkyns' history of Gloucestershire published in 1711 he notes the cost of the new parsonage at Adlestrop at £1500.[11] After that Broadwell was served by a succession of curates receiving the paltry sum of £32 a year in 1738. According to Mary Leigh's history, Mr Johnson was first in Adlestrop purely as a domestic chaplain at the Park but then 'he so greatly pleased our grandfather [Theophilus Leigh I] that upon hearing from a common friend of both, that he was singularly worthy, the Living was not divided, but given to Mr Johnson.' She also remembers 'there is still left a path, unploughed in Oddington field, called Dead Mans Ley; being the way in which Adlestrop formerly conveyed their dead to Broadwell.'[12]

In 1937 the rectory and all its glebe lands were sold in both Adlestrop and its neighbouring parish of Broadwell. The

Leighs bought the rectory from the Church Commissioners first for their own use and then, as it is now, to let via the Adlestrop Settlement as a private house. The Church built a new house for the curate at Broadwell which in 1960 became the rectory house for both parishes – reverting to the medieval system. The current rector of Adlestrop, a keen member of the local hunt, presides over seven parishes in the Evenlode Valley which besides Adlestrop include Broadwell, Oddington, Evenlode, Bledington, Icomb and Westcote.

Unlike his predecessors he receives his stipend from the Church of England and cannot rely on other sources of local income. A look at the records held in the Gloucestershire Archives certainly brings out the concerns of Jane's cousin two hundred years ago. Besides the business of the church, records show his correspondence about leases, tithes and local charities and how he also lent a helping hand to his neighbours and relatives with their business matters.

A bundle of documents underlines the importance of tithes. The tithe system had been in place since the ninth century and meant that a rector was owed a tenth of local farmers' produce. But for the clergy it was an issue fraught with difficulty as although it brought them close to their parishioners it also meant they were like the hated taxman. There was often confusion over whether landowners or their incumbments were due a tithe. At Stoneleigh for example the 'great tithes' which were the levies on cereal crops were owned by the Leighs of the Abbey, but the 'small tithes' taken from chickens, eggs and fruit were destined for the parish priest. At Adlestrop there was a huge kerfuffle about whether enclosed desmesne

'He really is engaged from morning to night.—There is no end to people's coming to him, on some pretence or other.—The magistrates, and overseers, and churchwardens are always wanting his opinion'. Mrs Elton on her husband's duties.
Emma

lands should bear a tithe or just a tithe of hay or none at all. A dispute arose when a tenant withheld £10 and the vicar took legal advice on whether this was actionable but there was no clear cut advice on the issue. However he was luckier with other landholdings. In 1763 he drew up an agreement with eight Adlestrop farmers for four-year leases of land on which they would pay rent and a tithe to him. The entries are precise: 'Thomas Tidmarsh occupying six yardlands and two cotlands shall yearly pay for tythe, the sum of fourteen pounds and ten pence'. The total amount raised from these eight farmers was £68 6s. 1d. The document is signed by all except two farmers who make a mark instead as they obviously could not write their names. All the sub-text of every Austen novel with its running theme of who is worth what and what they can expect in a will or from a living is summed up by these old scraps of papers with jottings totting up expected income and juggling figures; matters that Jane would have recognised from her own father's struggles to keep his head above water at Steventon. Mr Collins firmly believed that a rector's prime responsibility was that 'he must make such an agreement for tythes as may be beneficial to himself and not offensive to his patron.'

At Fanny Price's momentous first dinner party at the Grant's rectory, Dr Grant and Edmund become deep in a conversation which is overheard by Henry Crawford who tells his sister what they are discussing: 'The most interesting in the world...how to make money — how to turn a good income into a better.'

The Coopers were a large family of first cousins to Jane Austen who also embraced the church as their profession. Jane Leigh, Mrs Austen's sister, had married the Revd Dr Edward Cooper in 1768. His son, Mrs Austen's nephew, also called Edward, was educated at Eton and then at All Souls, Oxford. In 1799 we hear via a chatty letter of Jane's to her sister in January that:

Yesterday came a letter to my mother from Edward Cooper to announce, not the birth of a child, but of a living; for Mrs Leigh [The Hon. Mary Leigh of Stoneleigh] has begged his acceptance of the Rectory of Hamstall-Ridware in Staffordshire....we collect from his letter that he means to reside there, in which he shows his wisdom.

The estate at Hamstall Ridware had been acquired by the Stoneleigh Abbey Leighs in the early seventeenth century. Jane showed her approval that he would fulfil his clerical duties and not just be an absentee holder of the living. Jane goes on,

Staffordshire is a good way off; so we shall see nothing more of them till, some fifteen years hence, the Miss Coopers are presented to us, fine, jolly, handsome ignorant girls. The living is valued at 140 l. a year, but perhaps it may be improvable.[13]

Compare this with the living that Edmund can expect at Thornton Lacey of £700 a year or as Henry Crawford sees it, 'He will have a pretty income to make ducks and drakes with, and earned without much trouble...a fine thing for a younger brother.'

Edward Cooper was 'a notable exponent of the new trend'[14] known as Evangelism which Jane disapproved of, so perhaps this was another reason why the family had put off a journey to Staffordshire. Edward collected his sermons and had them published. One of them was designed especially for practical use in 'country congregations'; they were very successful and ran into many editions selling throughout the nineteenth century. Jane was always quite tart about him, disliking his sanctimonious ways – when he wrote to her about the birth of his baby son she wrote to Cassandra:

I have heard twice from Edward on the occasion, & his

letters have each been exactly what they ought to be–chearful & amusing.–He dare not write otherwise to *me*–but perhaps he might be obliged to purge himself from the guilt of writing Nonsense by filling his shoes with whole pease for a week afterward.[15]

The Evangelicals believed humanity needed to be 'born again' to overcome its evil nature – this was stressed in Edward Cooper's fourth book of sermons in which the topics of Regeneration and Conversion were paramount. This was not a view that Jane Austen adhered to. She believed that there was good and sometimes evil in everybody but that 'evil' ways could be shaken off if people considered their duty and accepted responsibilities. In *Mansfield Park* the characters of Henry and Mary Crawford are clearly shown to be morally flawed due to their lax upbringing and the poor example of their dissolute uncle. The same is true of Julia and Maria Bertram who 'had never been taught to govern their inclinations and tempers, by that sense of duty that alone can suffice'.

In 1801 Jane pokes fun at the idea of going into far-off Staffordshire:

Edward Cooper is so kind as to want us all to come to Hamstall this summer, instead of going to the sea, but we are not so kind as to mean to do it. The summer after, if you please, Mr Cooper, but for the present we greatly prefer the sea to all our relations.[16]

In fact the visit was put off until the year of 1806 when their stay at Adlestrop and Stoneleigh occurred. Adlestrop, being as it were, on the way from Bath to Staffordshire. It may have been at this time that she was able to visit Derbyshire and the Peak District and see 'all the celebrated beauties of Matlock, Chatsworth, Dovedale or the Peak'. Many commentators believe that Pemberley, the seat of Mr Darcy is based on

Chatsworth – although even Darcy's fortune would not be great enough for such an estate.

Edward Cooper attended the funeral of his patron, the Hon. Mary Leigh at Stoneleigh that fateful summer but then must have returned to Hamstall to await the Austens' party. On 23 August 1806 he wrote to Revd. Leigh and mentions the 'good health of all at Hamstall. Mrs C. with Mrs Austen and her Daughters unite with me in kind regards to yourself and Mrs E Leigh'.[17] Edward was obviously keen to be in the eye of all the beneficiaries at Stoneleigh when he wrote again to Joseph Hill on 26 September 1806 asking to be remembered to Mr Leigh Perrot. He also remarks that 'Mrs Austen and her daughters after staying with us for about five weeks, have left us for Southampton. They spoke with much pleasure of meeting you & Mrs Hill at Stoneleigh.' Jane caught whooping cough from one of his eight children and disliked the eldest boy whom she thought a bully. She wrote of him in 1809:

A great event happens this week at Hamstall, in young Edward's removal to school; he is going to Rugby & is very happy in the idea of it.–I wish his happiness may last, but it will be a great change, to become a raw school boy from being a pompous Sermon-Writer & a domineering Brother.[18]

When the terrible news came of Elizabeth Austen Knight's sudden death after the birth of her eleventh child, Jane first replied to Cassandra: 'Hamstall I suppose you write to yourselves'[19] but then perhaps had been asked to do it and reports two days later that she wrote to tell Edward Cooper and added that she hoped that he would not send 'one of his letters of cruel comfort to my poor brother'.[20] Jane worried that his piety would grate on her brother's nerves.

An excellent idea of Jane Austen's opinions on the accomplishments necessary for a member of the clergy come in a letter she wrote to the Prince Regent's librarian, the Revd James Stanier Clarke in 1815. This was a truly happy time for Jane who was enjoying popular success while nicely settled at Chawton. Clarke had met her while she was staying with Henry Austen in London and he had shown her around Carlton House, the Prince Regent's palatial mansion in St James's, and been most attentive – even offering her the use of his own library and apartments in Golden Square. More importantly he had, with the permission of the Prince Regent, arranged for her to dedicate *Emma* to the Regent. According to James Clarke, '...the Regent has read & admired all your publications'. He went on to beg Jane to turn her talents to:

> '...they [the Cooke cousins] admire *Mansfield Park* exceedingly...and the manner in which I treat the Clergy, delights them very much'
> Letter to Cassandra Austen, 14 June 1814

deliniate in some future Work the Habits of Life and Character and enthusiasm of a Clergyman—who should pass his time between the metropolis and the Country... Fond of, & entirely engaged in Literature—no man's enemy but his own. Pray dear Madam think of these things.[21]

Jane replied quite forthrightly declining the commission and explaining why:

The comic part of the character I might be equal to, but not the Good, the Enthusiastic, the Literary. Such a Man's Conversation must at times be on subjects of Science & Philosophy of which I know nothing...A Classical

Education, or at any rate, a very extensive acquaintance with English Literature, Ancient & Modern, appears to me quite Indispensable who wd do any justice to your Clergyman—And I think I may boast myself to be, with all possible Vanity, the most unlearned & uninformed Female who ever dared to be an Authoress.[22]

I find it rather touching how Jane looks up to those who have had a classical education, doubtless remembering her father, brothers and her cousins who could dispute on philosophy and quote from the ancients in the original Latin or Greek. However she might have mocked the Revd Clarke or others of the cloth, she was also sensible of the learning they had gained from their years at university. There is no bitterness in this acceptance of her 'ignorance' nor a wish to change the ways of the world so that a better education was made possible for a woman. The most Jane could and did do was to prick the pomposity of some of these men and quietly laugh at them through the lightness and fun of her fiction. Perhaps one can sum up the sort of faith or religious practice that Jane Austen admired by taking her description of Fanny Price's ideals as accurately perceived by Henry Crawford:

…he talked of her having such a steadiness and regularity of conduct, such a high notion of honour, and such an observance of decorum as might warrant any man in the fullest dependence on her faith and integrity, he expressed what was inspired by the knowledge of her being well principled and religious.

Henry Austen characterised his sister not long after her death as 'thoroughly religious and devout, fearful of giving offence to God, and incapable of feeling it towards any fellow creature'. This was a little sweeping but sums up her lifetime of regular attendance at church, formal devotions in the home and the composing of prayers. While she might amuse herself and her readers by her gentle teasing of clergymen and their eccentricities and failings, she never showed anything but acceptance of belief and a calm joy in her Christian faith.

CHAPTER ELEVEN

Warren Hastings and Jane Austen

'And Mr. Hastings! I am quite delighted with what such a man writes about it. Henry sent him the books after his return from Daylesford... I long to have you hear Mr. H's opinion of P & P. His admiring my Elizabeth so much is particularly welcome to me...' **Jane Austen in a letter to Cassandra, 15-16 September 1813**

A series of curious connections and coincidences brought together Warren Hastings, one of the most renowned men in England, and Jane Austen, the acclaimed author.

First of all the Leighs and their location in Adlestrop played a pivotal role as Warren Hastings had been brought up in the vicinity. The Hastings family and their ancestors had owned the lands and estate of Daylesford, a village less than a mile away from Adlestrop, until just before his birth and naturally regularly socialised with the Leighs. Warren Hastings had enjoyed a glittering career in India where he worked his way up from being a humble clerk in the East India Company to become the first governor-general of India. In 1785 he resigned and returned to England, not to a hero's welcome but instead to find himself impeached on charges of high crimes, misdemeanours and corruption although he had achieved more than any other Englishman to ensure the British remained in ascendance in India. His seven-year trial in Westminster Hall became a *cause célèbre* among the upper classes; the Queen,

Fanny Burney and a host of others attended its first day and watching the proceedings became a form of fashionable entertainment. In 1789 for example, a year after the trial had begun, Agnes Witts on a visit to London, noted in her diary:

> Rather a disagreeable Day, from a strong east wind, which made the dust dreadfull went at 11 o'clock to Hastinge's Trial, sat two hours before any thing began & and then not gratified either by the trial or appearance...[1]

Both the Leighs and the Austens would have followed the trial's course and rejoiced at Hastings' final acquittal. But before exploring Warren Hastings' local ties in Gloucestershire, let us also examine his links with the Austens which came through Jane's aunt, the memorably named Philadelphia Austen who went to India in search of a husband.

Philadelphia and her brother, George, had been brought up mainly by their uncle, Francis Austen, as their mother had died in childbirth while they were very young. In this respect, their upbringing resembled that of Warren Hastings whose parents had died during his childhood and he was initially brought up by poor and sometimes reluctant relatives until helped to a decent education by his uncle. George Austen was able to go to Oxford and be ordained but Philadelphia, however bright and agreeable she was, had few hopes of marriage proposals without a dowry.

A drastic solution seemed to be called for and was found. In the course of his work as a solicitor, Francis Austen acted for Tysoe Saul Hancock (1723-75), a surgeon in the employ of the East India Company. Apart from his profession Hancock augmented his income by trading Indian gems which he sent to Francis to resell in Britain on his behalf. Did Dr Hancock tell Francis Austen that he was looking out for a suitable wife?

However it may have been arranged, Philadelphia was adventurous enough and perhaps desperate enough, to take up this opportunity and make the long and perilous journey by sea to India. Although Hancock was not a tremendous catch for Philadelphia, he would be prepared to overlook her straitened circumstances.

> '...to a Girl of any Delicacy, the voyage in itself, since the object of it is so universally known, is a punishment that needs no other to make it very severe'
> *Catharine*

Jane Austen's unfinished novel, *Catharine,* which she wrote while still a teenager, alludes to this common practice whereby penniless young women went to hunt for a husband in India. In this extract the young lady described is the eldest daughter of a clergyman whose death has necessitated the dispersal of the family:

> The eldest daughter had been obliged to accept the offer of one of her cousins to equip her for the East Indies, and tho' infinitely against her inclinations had been necessitated to embrace the only possibility that was offered to her, of a Maintenance....her personal Attractions had gained her a husband as soon as she had arrived at Bengal...united to a man of double her own age.[2]

Philadelphia journeyed to India in 1751 on the *Bombay Castle* along with eleven other single women to a destination where the number of men seeking a European wife was considerable and the odds of securing a proposal of marriage would be in their favour. After a long voyage of eight months, aged just twenty-one, Philadelphia landed in Madras with a mixture of hope and apprehension. Six months later in February 1753, she married Dr Hancock.

In 1759 the Hancocks moved to Bengal which was where they first came across Warren Hastings. Ninety years later, the great Victorian historian George Macaulay would say: 'I think Hastings, though far from faultless, one of the greatest men England ever produced. He had pre-eminent talents for government, and great literary talents too...' Hastings had, through hard work and learning Hindustani, Persian and Bengali, become invaluable to the East India Company. He immersed himself in Indian culture and used his knowledge to strengthen the hold the British were gaining over India by working with the Indians rather than against them. He was quick-witted, small and lithe and a bundle of energy and, at the age of twenty-seven, just two years older than Philadelphia when they first met.

It was a tragic time for Warren Hastings whose wife and new baby daughter had just died, leaving his infant son, George, motherless. The boy stayed with his father but it was a time of political turmoil and danger in India and he decided to safeguard the life of his only son by sending him with a trusted companion on the long sea voyage to England. He had heard from Philadelphia about her brother and perhaps about his intended marriage to Cassandra Leigh and thought them an ideal couple to care for his child. He was never to see him again. Ostensibly the boy was sent as a pupil but because of his tender age later naturally fell more under the charge of Mrs Austen and, when he died of 'a putrid sore throat'(probably diphtheria), she must have grieved over his death as much as his own father was to.

According to the memoir written by Jane's descendants, William and Richard Arthur Austen-Leigh, the boy was a companion on the couple's brief honeymoon in 1764.[3]

The pair are believed to have had an unusual companion for such an occasion – namely, a small boy, six years old, the only son of Warren Hastings by his first wife. We are told that he was committed to the charge of Mr Austen when he was sent over to England in 1761...but a three-year-old boy is a curious charge for a bachelor, and poor little George must have wanted a nurse rather than a tutor. In any case he came under Mrs Austen's maternal care, who afterwards mourned for his early death 'as if he had been a child of her own.'

—◄•►—

In 1761 the Hancocks had their own child after a union of eight years, a little girl called Elizabeth, first known as Betsy and then as she grew older, Eliza. As noted in *Northanger Abbey* '...what young lady of common gentility will reach the age of sixteen without altering her name as far as she can?' Hastings became her godfather and settled the enormous gift of five thousand pounds on her. In India there was gossip and raised eyebrows about the relationship between Hastings and Philadelphia. Lord Clive wrote to his wife that Philadelphia had 'abandoned herself to Hastings' and advised her to avoid any friendship with Mrs Hancock.[4] But this may have been just malicious gossip as the friendship between Dr Hancock and Hastings continued and also extended to a business trading partnership in salt, timber, carpets and opium.[5] In all of the diaries and private papers of Warren Hastings there is nothing to back up this rumour. Hastings was known by all for his impetuous generosity to old friends, servants and anyone in need. He had numerous god-children who enjoyed his liberality and he fully supported the sons and nieces of his second wife, Marian.

The Hancocks, their daughter and Hastings, along with their Indian servants, all returned to England together in 1765 and it was only then that Hastings learnt of the sad death of his son. Once in England Hancock realised his savings from India were not adequate to support his family and he was forced to return east in 1768 leaving Philadelphia and their daughter in London. Sadly the family would never be reunited. Warren Hastings also resumed his life in India and Philadelphia kept up a correspondence with him with Hancock obligingly forwarding her letters. During this period, Philadelphia, on hearing Hastings had met a new woman, wanted to return to India but her husband vetoed the proposal. When she also suggested that Eliza should visit Bengal he told her that it was out of the question as the place had become 'lewd'. His closing remark was a gentle rebuke: 'You yourself know how impossible it is for a young girl to avoid being attracted to a young handsome man whose address is agreeable to her.'[6]

Naturally Philadelphia often took young Betsy to Hampshire to visit her brother and his children at Steventon. Betsy was a spirited and pretty girl who soon became a pet of the Austen family although her aunt found her a little spoilt. News of Dr Hancock's death in 1775 reached Philadelphia some six months afterwards along with the unhappy fact that he had left little money for her or Betsy. Into this breach stepped Warren Hastings, the executor of Hancock's will, who gave ten thousand pounds to the young widow to help support her. Whatever the reason for this gift, it left Philadelphia a rich and independent woman. Still keen to try pastures new she decided in 1780 to take herself and her lively daughter of nineteen, now always known as Eliza, to Paris to experience all the delights that living in the elegant capital could bring to them both. Jane would have been only five years old when they left but she had strong memories of her aunt and her vibrant cousin and despite the distance between them the intertwining of the two families continued.

Eliza's reputation as a rich heiress with a connection to Warren Hastings greatly increased her marriage prospects and in 1781, she married a dashing Frenchman, the Comte de Feuillide. The news concerned George Austen hugely as he feared that both his sister and her daughter would be 'giving up their friends, their country and their religion'. But when Eliza was expecting her first child in 1786 both she and her husband wanted the birth to be in London. Philadelphia and Eliza took a house in Orchard Street for that purpose and the child, who was safely delivered, was named Hastings de Feuillide, in honour of his mother's godfather.

The child was introduced to Warren Hastings and his second wife Marian when Eliza and her mother spent a three week visit at their house in Windsor after his return to England.

Mother and child remained in England and it was soon apparent that the boy was both mentally and physically disabled although Eliza never acknowledged this openly in her letters; with the help of her mother and servants she was able to resume her love of theatre visits and dancing. Eliza was a social butterfly who moved in the top circles in both Paris and London but she never forgot her country cousins. At Christmas in 1787 she stayed in Steventon (they could only have friends and relations to stay in the holidays when all the boy boarders were at home on their holidays) and suffused the whole family with her love of amateur dramatics. The great barn opposite the rectory was fitted out as a theatre and one can imagine Jane, then aged twelve, taking a keen interest in all the excitement of the occasion. She must have been dazzled by her exotic cousin, married to a French count and a frequenter of high society.

'Cassandra & Jane are both very much grown (The latter is now taller than myself)...My Heart gives preference to Jane, whose kind partiality to me, indeed requires a return of the same nature.'

Letter from Eliza 1792

In July 1788 Mr and Mrs Austen, Cassandra and Jane stayed with Eliza in London and in August Eliza visited Oxford where both of Jane's elder brothers, James and Henry, escorted her. They vied for the attention of their flirtatious cousin who professed herself enchanted with the delightful gardens at St John's College and wished she could be a Fellow and enjoy it every day.

Part of Eliza's character, to my mind, lives on in the portrayal of Mary Crawford in *Mansfield Park*. She is described as having a 'lively dark eye, clear brown complexion and general prettiness'. Mary Crawford instantly gives her agreement to the idea of putting on an amateur production at Mansfield Park while Sir Thomas Bertram is away on business in the West Indies. She 'hopes to be admitted into the company and will be happy to take the part of any old Duenna or tame Confidante…'. This announcement is enough to convince the staid Edmund that he must drop his own objections to avoid any outsiders joining the cast. Eliza, like Mary Crawford played the harp, she disliked the country and loved town life and made no secret of her love of money and comfort. The part of Amelia that Mary is to play in *Mansfield Park* is described by Julia Bertram in a fit of pique as 'An odious, little, pert, unnatural, impudent girl'. It is a part made for flirting – an art that Eliza excelled in. Jane Austen also put into Mary Crawford's mouth many remarks about her dislike of clergymen and the Church. Perhaps Eliza had said these things in jest to her uncle, George Austen, or to her cousins.

> '…immediately paying a visit to Steventon, because my Uncle informs us, that Midsummer & Christmas are the only Seasons when his Mansion is sufficiently at liberty to admit of his receiving his Friends'
> *Letter from Eliza, 23 May 1786*

Life for Eliza and the Comte changed abruptly in 1789 with the terrifying news of the French Revolution. The Comte received letters from France threatening him with the confiscation of his estates if he did not return. The danger was immense and the Comte paid with his life in his struggle to retain his inheritance. He met his fate at the guillotine on 12 February 1794. The event caused shock waves at the heart of the family circle and its ripples must have reached all the way to the Austens. Eliza's grief at losing her husband in this brutal manner can only be imagined.

In 1795 Eliza's generous godfather was finally acquitted of all charges after England's longest political trial. Henry Austen penned a rather awkward letter to him:

> Dear Sir,
> A humble and hitherto silent spectator of national concerns, permit me at the present interesting moment to transgress the strictness of propriety, and though without permission, I hope without offence to offer you the warm & respectful congratulations of a heart deeply impressed with a sense of all you have done & suffered.

Henry also referred to the 'many instances of your kindness shown to me'[7] and obviously wanted to remind Warren Hastings of his existence because he had determined to ask his fair cousin Eliza to be his wife. She turned him down at first but their courtship continued until she succumbed in 1797 knowing that he was fond of her son as well as herself. When Eliza wrote of her marriage to her godfather she stressed this point:

> ...for some time in Possession of a comfortable Income, and the excellence of his Heart, Temper and Understanding, together with steady attachment to me, his Affection for my little Boy, and disinterested concurrence in the disposal of my Property in favor of this latter, have at length induced me to an acquiescence which I have withheld for more than two years.[8]

Henry, who had been a captain in the Oxfordshire Militia, left the army and set up in partnership as a banker. He and Eliza lived in some style in Upper Berkeley Street where they enjoyed London life and lived beyond their means; her trust fund from Warren Hastings had long been used up. In 1801 her sickly son, Hastings, died at the age of fifteen and some months after his death Henry wrote again to Warren Hastings to ask for financial help but was refused. Perhaps he felt he had done enough and that now happily married again he wanted all memories of his connections to Philadelphia quietly passed over. Despite this refusal Warren Hastings had helped Frank Austen at George Austen's request during the years of his trial by putting Frank in touch with some valuable connections at the East India Company. The upshot of this was that Frank became profitably involved in transporting silver from China via Madras to England while the Navy turned a blind eye. It did not seem to harm Frank's eventual climb to become Admiral of the Fleet.[9]

After its publication Henry sent a copy of *Pride and Prejudice* to Warren Hastings at Daylesford and showed Jane the thanks he received in which Hastings praised the book. She was very pleased and in a letter to Cassandra on 15 September 1813 writes:

> And Mr. Hastings! I am quite delighted with what such a man writes about it. Henry sent him the books after his return from Daylesford... I long to have you hear Mr. H's opinion of P & P. His admiring my Elizabeth so much is particularly welcome to me...[10]

Later in that letter she also remarks that Henry had not been able to give Hastings copies of S&S (*Sense and Sensibility*) as 'The Books came to hand too late for him to have time for it, before he went.'

Jane was basing her high opinion of Warren Hastings not only because of his fame but because, I believe, she would have met him face to face during her stays at Adlestrop. The two villages are within a mile of each other and their parishes are twinned for local government purposes. The great house that

Warren Hastings built for himself still survives and the Daylesford Estate is today owned by one of the richest men in England, Sir Anthony Bamford. It

'...the Country about it is exceedingly pretty and affords a great variety of delightful Walks'
Letter from Eliza de Feuillide on a visit to Daylesford, 4 August 1797

is a short walk from Adlestrop via various footpaths to the grounds of the house and the upmarket set of old barns which have been transformed into a chic shop, café and health spa known as Daylesford Organics.

Mary Leigh in her memoir talks about a branch of the Hastings family having lived in a house in Blundells Field, Adlestrop in the seventeenth century and that 'they were most likely a collateral branch of the Daylesford family of Hastings, who are very ancient in this neighbourhood'.[11] The friendship between the Leighs and Hastings' family went back a long way. Theophilus Leigh I regularly met up with, 'his contemporaries & great friends, the Juxons, Penystons, Hastings and Jones's. Mr Parsons (the Adlestrop curate) read the weekly *Courant*, and over it they certainly drank excreable wine and probably talked wicked Treason.'[12]

This Hastings was probably Warren's grandfather who was an Oxford graduate and became the rector at Daylesford. Mary Leigh describes how the Daylesford estate fell out of the family's hands until repurchased by Warren Hastings.

As a small boy Warren Hastings had dreamt of regaining his ancestors' lands and when he came back to England as a rich grandee, despite having a mansion in St James's Square and a base in Windsor, set about realising his vision by buying the manor of Daylesford. He had been born nearby in the Oxfordshire village of Churchill where his father, Penyston Hastings was curate. His mother, Hester Warren died shortly after his birth in 1732 and Penyston remarried and then voyaged to Barbados taking all the money from his children's trust funds with him. Warren stayed in the country with his grandfather and great-aunt Elizabeth in reduced circumstances. All the family were keenly aware how far the Hastings family had fallen after having owned the Daylesford Estate since early Medieval and Tudor times – it was only early in the eighteenth-century that his great-grandfather had been forced to sell the house to Jacob Knight, a London merchant. Warren's route out of rural poverty came when his uncle Howard sent him first to a boarding school and then, in 1743, to one of the best public schools in England: Westminster. Late in his life he recalled his childish hopes as he sat by the bank of Kingham Brook near Churchill:

'One of the greatest and best of men -- & how he has been rewarded? By nine years impeachment and Parliamentary persecution.' *Mary Leigh in her Family History*

> To lie beside the margin of that stream, and muse, was one of my favourite recreations; and there, one bright summer's day, when I was scarcely seven years old, I well remember that I first formed the determination to purchase back Daylesford.[13]

Warren Hastings made wholesale improvements to the Daylesford Estate probably spurred on by his Leigh neighbours. One of the first places he went to after his return to England in 1785 was Adlestrop where he stayed in August with Thomas Leigh at the Parsonage and noted in his diary how he 'rode over all the grounds of Daylesford before breakfast'.[14]

Although the trial had ruined him financially he had generous help from the East India Company and had to give the officials there an explanation for his expenditure:

> In 1789, I purchased the principal part of Daylesford, and about two years since the remainder; it was an object that I had long wished to possess; it was the spot in which I had

passed much of my infancy; and I feel for it an affection of which an alien could not be susceptible, because I see in it attractions which that stage of my life imprinted on my mind, and my memory still retains. It had been the property of my family during many centuries, and had not been more than seventy-five years out of their possession. I should not notice these trivial circumstances, but that detailing the process of my expenses, I feel that this part of them which relates to this place, I have to defend myself, if I can, against the charge of extravagance, and I fear I have no better excuse to make for it.[15]

The sum of £54,400 is given as the amount spent on the purchase and improvement of the Daylesford Estate. The indefatigable Agnes Witt recorded the beginnings of the work at Daylesford in her diary in October 1789:

...the Gentlemen went to a Land Tax meeting at Chip: & I took Mrs Western to visit both the Houses of Leigh at Adlestrop, going by the way to survey Mr Hastings' great works & improvements at Dailsford, a fine situation but a great undertaking to go thro it.[16]

A new house was built and designed by the architect Samuel Pepys Cockerell who, although he later became famous for his Indian-style motifs at Sezincote outside nearby Moreton in Marsh, avoided anything so obvious at Daylesford. The only trace of Indian influence at Daylesford House is the top of its dome and a marble interior fireplace which shows a Hindu sacrifice and is supported by carvings of Indian women on each side. It was a grand house that was run by seven men servants and six maids together with gardeners and grooms and no expense was spared in making it luxurious and fashionable. There were eight carriage horses, ten farm horses and three dogs. The golden Cotswold stone was quarried near the villages of Windrush and Barrington and artisans from London lived nearby for a year or more painting the cornices and window shutters in shades of rose pink and green, gilding the interior and applying special paint effects to doors and window frames. The Birmingham Soho factory furnished the wrought iron embellishments and the tiles were, of course, Wedgwood. Innovations of plate glass, a Bramah WC and a hot bath were all installed.

The gardens were landscaped by the architect and garden designer, John Davenport, complete with artificial lake, walled garden and Gothic orangery. They have been improved and restored by the present owners and are open under the National Gardens Scheme for charity a couple of times a year. In 1788-89 Hastings spent almost five hundred pounds for spruce, silver firs, Lombardy poplars, hornbeams and walnut trees, scented lilac bushes, exotic juniper and acacia, feathery tamarisk and tulip trees, heliotropes and creamy magnolias to make the grounds a delightful haven. The Orangery was stocked with exotic fruits whose seeds were supplied from India. Custard apples, lychees, alligator pears (the old name for avocados) and mangoes flourished while in the Walled Garden a rich crop of peaches, cherries, nectarines, plums, strawberries, raspberries, gooseberries, currants and grapes kept Hastings and his guests well fed. In *Mansfield Park* even Mrs Norris at the vicarage plants an apricot tree against the shelter of a stable wall although Dr Grant complains its fruits are insipid and uneatable. Mrs Norris protests 'Sir. It is a moor park...a present from Sir Thomas, but I saw the bill, and I know it cost seven shillings.'[17]

Hastings' flamboyance extended to importing Tibetan goats and yaks and cattle from Bhutan to cross with the native animals.[18] The Estate was not just for pleasure but for farming with about 100 acres of arable land, 250 sheep and twenty cows. His Arab stallion sired many foals and there were up to thirty horses grazing the green fields.

In 1797 Eliza visited Daylesford after staying at the spa town of Cheltenham and wrote to her cousin:

> One of my principal inducements for coming here was the neighbourhood of my old Friends the Hastings's whom I am just returned from visiting. They have got a place called Daylesford, which is one of the most beautiful I ever saw…the Park and Grounds are really a little Paradise, and that the House is fitted up with a degree of Taste & Magnificence seldom to be met with[19]

Eliza and Henry visited Daylesford together in August 1808 and this was the last time her name appears in Hastings's diaries.

History relates that Warren Hastings had the old stones, some possibly still upright, known as the Grey Geese of Adlestrop taken down from Adlestrop Hill and used to form some ornamental rock work in his grounds and to make an island in his lake. There are still many old stones lying in the grass on that hill near the old ruined Iron Age burial mounds and also on the other side of the road near Chastleton camp. A legend relates that these stones were turned from geese into stone by an old witch as they were grazing without permission. Another theory is that perhaps they were all part of a very ancient stone avenue leading to the Rollright Stones that are, as the crow flies, a couple of miles away on a hill crest.

'A clerk of Oxenford', who paid a visit to Hastings at Daylesford, wrote a ballad, in 1808, in honour of the Grey Geese, and contributed it to the *Gentleman's Magazine*. Having related how the old woman who looked after the geese was treated by the witch, the poet proceeded to say, that she was offered some consolation for the loss of her geese by the following prediction :

But pitying fate at length shall abate
The rigour of this decree,
By the aid of a sage in a far distant age
And he comes from the East country.

A Pundit his art to this seer shall impart,
Where'er he shall wave his wand,
The hills shall retire, and the valleys aspire,
And the waters usurp the land.

Then Alice thy flock their charm shall unlock,
And pace with majestic stride
From Adlestrop heath to Daylesford beneath,
To lave in their native tide

The church at Daylesford was rebuilt by Hastings in 1816 and he was buried there two years afterwards. An elegant Coade-stone monumental funerary urn marks his grave in the churchyard with the spare inscription 'Warren Hastings 1818'. Neither he nor the Austens would recognise much of the village or the church today. The church was completely rebuilt in its present high Gothic style in 1860 for Harman Grisewood, the owner of Daylesford at that time. All the old houses in the village were pulled down one by one and together with the lodges, one of which still remains on the main road where the footpath leads to Adlestrop, were replaced by Grisewood. They all resemble each other with strong Victorian gothic features.

The Leighs must have been delighted to have Warren Hastings and his second wife, Marian, as their neighbours. I am sure the Austens would have been asked to call at Daylesford on their Gloucestershire trips. Would Warren not have wanted to see Mrs Austen – the last person to see his young son George alive, and talk to her about his memories of the boy? The family would have either taken her cousin's carriage or walked the short distance across the fields to the mansion. I can imagine him showing Jane and her mother all the improvements to the grounds, the house and the church.

In 1808 Jane alluded in a typically facetious comparison to a painting that hung in the Picture Room at Daylesford which reminded Jane of a recent journey Cassandra had made to the Isle of Wight from Southampton: 'I cannot help thinking and re-thinking of your going to the Island so heroically. It puts me in mind of Mrs Hastings' journey down the Ganges…'[20]

This dramatic incident was painted by William Hodges after a commission from Warren Hastings. It depicted Mrs Hastings' perilous 400-mile trip down the Ganges in 1782 in order to nurse him back to health. The painting entitled *Storm on the Ganges: Mrs Hastings at the Rocks of Colgong*[21] shows a stormy scene with billowing dark clouds lit up with a double rainbow under which a fragile Indian boat is buffeted by the tempestuous waters of the great river – a far cry from Cassandra's actual trip across the more tranquil Solent. From this letter it is obvious that both sisters were quite familiar with the interior of Daylesford and been told the history and significance of the painting. A copy of the scene was also etched on glass which hung in the house.

Jane concluded her remarks by adding '…& if we had but a room to retire into to eat our fruit, we wd have a picture of it hung there.' An allusion to all the exotic fruits from the Orangery which visitors would have eaten or been given as gifts to take back to the Rectory kitchen.

In *Mansfield Park* the Bertram sisters complain to their aunt Norris about the ignorance of their cousin Fanny:

> But, aunt, she is really so very ignorant! – Do you know, we asked her last night, which way she would go to get to Ireland; and she said, she should cross to the Isle of Wight. She thinks of nothing but the Isle of Wight, and she calls it *the Island*, as if there were no other island in the world.

Hampshire people and those actually living on the Isle of Wight still call it 'the Island' today.

———

Warren Hastings took his duties as chief landowner of Daylesford very seriously, looking after the sheep shearers, the maid servants and the day labourers. A parish green was created and he had two cottages built for widows. He went to the meetings of the turnpike commissions at Stow on the Wold writing in his diary: 'dined at the Stow club, and rode home afterwards with Mr Penyston'. It was obviously a dull occasion and he added, 'NB to order my horse next time at 7, or before'.[22] In 1815 he gave the whole parish a dinner to celebrate the peace in Europe after Wellington's victory at Waterloo. We know from his diary that Warren Hastings frequently visited both Adlestrop and Stoneleigh to call on the Leighs – here is a typically brief entry that he wrote in the last year of his life: 'Feb. 19th. I visited Adlestrop and my neighbours, and returned by Daylesford church, not apparently worse; but after dinner my cough caused incessant irritation.'

His cough may have proved fatal to the old Nabob as he died just six months after this on 22 August 1818 at the age of eighty-six. Abraham Newman, one of the Adlestrop villagers, was taken to his funeral by his parents, probably with many others, – this was family lore recorded by his great-granddaughter who was born and brought up in the village in the 1920s. Marian Hastings survived him until her death in 1837, her son Charles (from her first marriage) and his wife lived there until 1853. On Charles' death the house and its contents were sold and dispersed.

Eliza de Feuillide, then Eliza Austen, died in the same year that *Pride and Prejudice* was published in April 1813. Jane left Chawton with Henry to nurse her on her deathbed. Eliza was buried alongside her mother and son in Hampstead.

CHAPTER TWELVE

Adlestrop Now

'Yes, I remember Adlestrop, the name…' **Edward Thomas**
'Adlestrop'

If Jane Austen were to return to the village today how much of it would she recognise? Not just its physical appearance but its day-to-day life and the existence of its inhabitants?

Adlestrop is a very compact village which has a strong sense of its identity and fosters strong feelings of belonging. This may be due to the Leigh family retaining it as an estate village over so many centuries. It was not until the mid-1990s that a change in the law made it possible for those who owned houses on long leases to buy their freeholds. The government of the day changed the leasehold laws mainly to help urban dwellers living in large blocks of flats who held long leases. However, thanks to a resident of Adlestrop and the offices of the local Member of Parliament, the question of rural leases was debated and the laws were amended to allow freeholds to be purchased from the Trustees of the Adlestrop Settlement. This has created a new dimension to the dynamics of the village with a split between those who own their houses and others who rent them on short-term leases. But it is a positive change and has resulted in greater diversity among the residents. The village is also fortunate that all the houses are usually fully occupied, there are no 'holiday' lets and very few 'weekenders'.

Adlestrop is on the edge of the largest AONB – an Area

Adlestrop today

of Outstanding Natural Beauty – in England and Wales. Over forty per cent of the area looked after by the Cotswold District Council is within this AONB and its purpose is 'to ensure the conservation and enhancement of the natural beauty of the Cotswolds'. This AONB was first designated in the 1960s and extended in 1990 and has undoubtedly helped to shield the countryside around Adlestrop from modern developments. The landscape around the village is still beautiful and unspoilt. Jane Austen, a great walker herself, would be delighted to see how many ramblers take to the well-kept footpaths and bridleways that criss-cross the vicinity. The village lies exactly on some long-distance paths such as the Diamond Way which is a sixty-mile circuit of the northern Cotswolds, and the Macmillan Way which starts in Boston, Lincolnshire and wends some three hundred miles through the Cotswolds via Stow and Tetbury to the destinations of either Abbotsbury in Dorset or Barnstaple in Devon.

In Jane Austen's time the requirements of the picturesque were not designated by laws and local authorities but by fashionable arbiters of taste. The Cotswolds would not have been deemed a place of outstanding natural beauty – eighteenth-century perceptions preferred more dramatic landscapes such as the Alps, the Lake District or the Peak District. The area was commonly thought of as an exceptionally backward and rural region famous for its yokels.

It is an entertaining exercise to walk around Adlestrop and see how many of the buildings remain from when Jane Austen walked its paths and how much is new. If we start a perambulation with our backs to the church we can explore how the succeeding two centuries have altered the village. Opposite the church is the old gabled rectory, built in 1672 with eight hearths. It was not markedly different from the rectory at Steventon which had two square windows either side of the front door and three above. Here at Adlestrop two bays were added in the late nineteenth century which upsets its symmetry – just the sort of thing that General Tilney abhorred: '...if there's one thing more another my aversion , it is a patched-on bow.' It is probable that its interior was superior to the rectory at Steventon which was plainly whitewashed and the rooms left without the embellishment of cornices and, according to her nephew, 'furnished with less elegance than would now be found in most ordinary dwellings'. All we know for certain of the interior of the rectory at Adlestrop was that Mary Leigh's bedroom was covered in a Chinese-style wallpaper – a fashion that was all the rage then, but we do know that Revd Thomas Leigh, Jane's host, was wealthy enough to employ a butler and two liveried manservants, plus five maids who also lived in the house, which seems to indicate a comfortable lifestyle. This is where Jane Austen stayed, now a private house, still rented from the Adlestrop Estate on a lease and renamed Adlestrop House since it ceased being a rectory. A smart gravel sweep lies behind the gates leading to a portico and pillared entrance which was restored to the present site in the nineteenth century after the Reverend had earlier changed its position to the side of the house to face the best view towards the 'Little Lake'. You can see on the right of the house outbuildings with a pigeon loft and the old stables. Behind these is a huge square of ground, now laid to grass, which was probably once part of the Revd Thomas' walled vegetable garden. The grounds to the side of the house are immaculately kept. All of this Jane would have enjoyed after her cousin's landscaping in the 1770s but, as shown in Chapter Six, the walk around the lawns down to the larger lake no longer exists. The little lake and the stream have been dredged and tidied up for boating, fishing and swimming and the pretty wooden bridge over the brook which links the shrubbery at the top of the great meadow has been repaired. On the bridleway a deep hedge has been planted which visually reinforces the divide between the old rectory and Adlestrop Park undoing the plans of Repton. The most important and drastic change to Adlestrop was to the bridleway itself, once the main road along which the Austen's coach and horses would have travelled direct to the rectory's door. All was altered in the Leigh's rush to improvement in the 1800s under Repton's guidance leading to the construction of the present road lay-out.

Overlooking the old rectory is the church where attendance at the two regular monthly services, apart from the Harvest Festival and the candlelit Christmas Carol Services, is often in single figures. Despite this, pride is taken in the upkeep of the churchyard and a rota of volunteers mows the grass throughout the summer months. One end of the ground is kept untouched allowing wild flowers and insects to flourish; it is threaded with primroses in the spring and buttercups and clover in high summer. By the church gate is a topiary yew cross carefully kept, as are the red rose bushes on either side of the path.

You enter the church through the door in the west tower, past the font to the pews. Outside a yew tree offers shade and along the high back wall of the churchyard which James Leigh erected is the ironwork gate to Adlestrop Park, now permanently padlocked. The Leigh vault is under the south transept and outside there is a small railed enclosure containing a fine memorial vase decorated with a Greek key pattern on a grooved pillar next to a tomb marked with an ornate carved cross but it is now impossible to read their inscriptions. However I believe they must be to Theophilus Leigh and his wife Anne (see below). Inside are more Leigh memorials on the floor, and on the walls plus their coats of arms on the hatchments. The most poignant is to the left of the church altar, which was put in place by Mary Leigh (the wife of the Revd Thomas) and her sister Cassandra Cooke which tells us that their parents, Theophilus Leigh (the Master of Balliol) and his wife Anne Bee are interred 'enclosed within an iron rail' plus the remains of other Leighs, Cookes and Bees – some of whom had died as 'infants'. At the end of this sad list the memorial states: 'Circles tho' small are complete'.

Jane would have sat in the pews in the north transept which were reserved for the rector's household listening to her cousin's sermons, while the south transept was for the lord of the manor. How often the rest of the pews were filled then we do not know although in 1851 it was said that 'all parishioners without exception' attended church at least once a week.[1]

The full peal of church bells cast in 1711 by Abraham Rudhall of Gloucester which Jane would have heard, have not been rung since 1989 due to damage to the bell frame but there is a campaign afoot to rehang them and for villagers to hear the bells again. The church clock which was added to celebrate

Queen Victoria's Golden Jubilee still chimes the hours and is only seen on the north and east side of the tower – these being the sides visible in the village .

Immediately opposite the church gate are attractive cottages with diamond-paned windows: Coachman's Cottage has a plaque above its front door dated 1722 and is probably older than the adjoining Old Schoolhouse judging from the stonework but at some point was refurbished to match its neighbour. The architectural historian David Verey believes the Schoolhouse was built in the mid-nineteenth century in the Tudor Revival style – perhaps designed by W.A. Nesfield who was working at Adlestrop Park in 1848.

A fascinating booklet by Rose Evelyn Cholmondeley, daughter of the Revd Henry Pitt Cholmondeley (who married a daughter of Lord Leigh), describing the inhabitants in 1876-77 records a Thomas and Sarah Wyatt and their son and daughter living there and next door in the schoolhouse the coachman 'of the house' (as opposed to the old rectory) with his wife and five children.[2] It was, after all, well into the twentieth century before cars would replace these men. Rose died in 1907 but her brother, Lionel, found her pencil jottings about 'Adlestrop, Its Cottages and their Inmates' in her papers and had 'these lively descriptions' transcribed and printed, together with some photographs, in a small hardback book in 1935. Rose was another vicar's daughter who took delight in observing and delivering her personal verdicts on her neighbours with no holds barred. Her vignettes of village life are by turns caustic and sympathetic.

The Old Schoolhouse was finally closed in 1916 and the children of Adlestrop went to Oddington and Evenlode instead. Now the local primary schools are in Bledington, Kingham and Stow and there are two good state secondary schools in Bourton-on-the-Water and Chipping Campden. Looking back to the eighteenth century, education for village children was totally reliant on donations from the rich; in Adlestrop Joanna

Brandis left £100 for putting the poor children of Adlestrop to school and the money was entrusted to the lord of the manor to pay out. This charity still exists and Lord Leigh is still its trustee. In 1790 there was a day school supported by private charity with donations from the Leighs and other local gentry. In 1803 the school was attended by sixteen children who were taught to read and knit among other things and was described as a school of industry. By 1818 there was a day school for eighteen boys and another for twenty-six girls and a Sunday school which had an attendance of fifty-two children – a small bequest made by Revd Thomas Leigh on his death in 1813 helped run this.[3] The two separate schools for boys and girls were later combined and the new building on the current site was built. So although Jane Austen would not have seen this particular building she would have seen (and heard) the comings and goings at the first school and observed its pupils. The life and bustle of the school is long departed; how quiet and uneventful earlier inhabitants would find the village street now – it is impossible to imagine Adlestrop so full of children playing and running to and from their homes. At harvest time they would be out in the fields helping their parents and, even put on the payroll at a rate of sixpence a day. The parish records show that between 1780 and 1791 there were sixty-nine births in Adlestrop which included eleven children born to the extensive Newman clan of three married couples: Abraham and Mary, Richard and Hannah, and William and Sarah. In 1877 Rose Evelyn Cholmondeley mentions a Mrs Newman living in the back part of Manor House Farm to whom 'must be accorded the palm of being the best washerwoman in the village.'[4] The Newman family went on to run the post office notably Dorothy Price (née Newman) who did so for forty-seven years until her retirement in 1998 after taking over the reins from her mother; now her daughter-in-law has continued the family tradition and is currently postmistress.

I suspect the adjoining property to the Old Schoolhouse

(8-9 Main Street) is nineteenth century and would not have been there during Jane Austen's time. It has been fully modernised in the last three years, the leasehold sold to a new owner and new extensions and gardens laid out. Walking further down on the same side are some ugly garages and two modern houses, Apple Tree Cottage and Cottage on the Green, built in the late twentieth century of local stone on what remained of the green and what were once gardens belonging to the post office. Jane would have seen more open space and extensive gardens with large vegetable plots.

Before turning into Main Street it is best to retrace our footsteps and return to the right hand side of the church where the grounds of Adlestrop Park begin. They are seen best from the great meadow beyond its ha-ha or through the gate at the back of the churchyard where you can glimpse the Sanderson Miller frontage and the graceful Cedar of Lebanon (probably planted in 1848) on the front lawn. From the roadway a daunting security door between two great stone pillars bars the entrance via a small driveway to the portico of c.1700 which carries the Leigh's crest of unicorn heads. One can still appreciate its proximity to Jane's lodgings at the rectory, just a stone's throw away.

Robert Hartman, a children's writer, who lived at Adlestrop Park during the First World War when he was a teenager rhapsodised about the house and its views in his memoirs:

I do not think there exists anywhere in England a more delightful, medium-sized-to-largish country house than Adlestrop. The house...looks, from gently rising ground, across a diminutive park which contains immense elm trees, a cricket ground which is probably the most dangerous in England, and a lake fringed, at the far end, with beech trees, which are reflected in the water to form, in autumn, a double display of russet and gold. In the distance, silhouetted on the skyline, is the church tower of

Stow-in-the-Wold. If this is not the most beautiful view in the world, it is certainly the one that I love most.[5]

A man who could discuss the picturesque with the best of Jane Austen's characters! Hartman was also a keen sportsman and detailed the 'shoots' on the estate which had sufficient coverts to provide a two-day shoot for four or five guns. Partridges on 1 September were plentiful and a bag of thirty brace was the result of a day's shooting.

The present occupiers who have lived there since 1992 have spent much time and money on restoring the house and its gardens which had fallen into some disrepair. It was standing empty after being used as a school for delinquent boys between 1967 and 1989. All the unfortunate sheds and temporary classrooms erected around it have been removed and it is once more a splendid house with a huge kitchen garden and well-kept lawns enjoying panoramic views of the Evenlode Vale. Its extensive grounds and gardens once reached as far as Reality House (see below). There is an old ice house remaining which the Leighs must have used before refrigeration and several small stone built houses in the grounds plus tennis courts, stabling and a swimming pool. On the other side of the Park's drive, shielded by high walls and surrounded by mature trees, many of which were planted by Repton, is the old dovecote with a lantern and a Welsh slate roof. It has now been cleverly converted into a private house. In the spring its lawns are thick with snowdrops.

Next to the Dovecote's drive, facing the green and on a higher level is a row of five cottages – Stable Cottages – which are rented from the estate. These were once the old stables belonging to the Park and were turned into homes in the mid-1970s. Midway between the row the original buildings where the Leigh's coaches would have been kept still stand with their open arches. Some of the modern day occupants work at the racing stables at the bottom of the village. Adjacent to these and separated by a high wall is Manor Farm House (previously called Home Farm) built in the mid-eighteenth century which Jane would have seen, now occupied by one family but no longer anything to do with farming or the land. Just outside its gated side entrance is a huge topiary snail skilfully clipped which always amuses passers-by. From Manor Farm House can be seen, up a short driveway, in what were previously the walled kitchen gardens of Adlestrop Park, a modern mansion, Reality House, built in the 1970s. The old red brick wall of the former garden is still there along the drive and at the back of the house. Cherry trees were once espaliered along the wall, always netted against predatory birds to protect their fruit but, of course, they are long gone.

Continuing along Schooler's Lane the blacksmith's has disappeared and Smith's Barn, which was left derelict until the late twentieth century, has been converted into a comfortable home and has just had its garden stylishly redesigned with an avenue of silver birches, huge balls of box and a sunken garden among its features. Schooler's Lane follows the side of the old Cider Mill Orchard, an irregular shaped green space inhabited by a sole grey horse who roams under the few remaining apple trees. At the foot of the orchard is a small single-storied cottage, Warden's Cottage, its date unknown. It is near to New Road, also called Back Row by some and North Row by Rose Evelyn Cholmondeley. On one corner at the end of Schooler's Lane behind a high hedge, sits Orchard Cottage, a modern bungalow, built in the mid-1960s.

The terrace of four cottages was erected around 1800 by the Leighs intended for local tradesmen and labourers. The narrow lane here was constructed to facilitate access to the main turnpike towards Chipping Norton and to link up with Schooler's Lane. Jane would have definitely seen these new houses and heard all about their construction and the making of the new roads from the Leighs. Once again their entrances face away from the road.

The two farms on the hillside: Fern Farm and Hillside Farm (formerly Old Parsonage Farm) were occupied by tenant farmers and would have looked new to the Austens. Hill Barn and its cottages would also have been there – now they are in a ruinous state. Jane would have walked close to them if she went across the fields and over the hill to Chastleton to see the magnificent old Jacobean house owned by the Leigh's friends, the Jones's. Chastleton House and its garden are now owned by the National Trust and both are renowned for retaining their original Jacobean character and avoiding modernisation (unlike Adlestrop Park). The modern Macmillan Way footpath now guides walkers on this same route.

At the end of the village going towards Evenlode, stands the village hall which was built by a local benefactor in 1962 and the racing stables by Lower Farm House. There were cottages and an old mill near to the sharp bend in the road by Marsh Bridge where the Parish Brook re-emerges to wend its way across the fields but these were pulled down in the reorganisation of the roads in the 1800s. A public footpath follows the side of the brook. This spot is also known as the Wash Brook to those born and bred in the village.

Lower Farm House and the Granary, again mid-eighteenth century constructions, have both been extensively added to and modernised in recent years but still manage to fit in well and blend into the Cotswold scene. The fine flight of stone steps outside the Granary, remind one of its original usage as a safe place to store the harvest away from rats. In common with the rest of the village their inhabitants now have nothing to do with the land or agriculture. Lower Farm House was a thriving cattle farm right up to the 1960s boasting a herd of Herefords. New stock would arrive on trucks which stopped at Adlestrop Station to be herded up the street to the farm and milk churns were loaded on and off the local train network from the farm.

Jane may have walked either along the pathway by the parish brook or alongside the new road perhaps as far as

Evenlode village, or turned left at the T-junction towards the turnpike road and Tolsey Cottage to reach the large lake and walk back beside the river or through the meadow, with its young elms, oaks and beech trees just planted by Repton, scattering the bleating sheep, home to the Rectory, enjoying the splendid vista of Adlestrop Park's frontage above its ha-ha. The Macmillan Way takes ramblers along here. The lodge at the side of the park post-dates Jane Austen's era as does the cricket pavilion and ground. It is very likely that there were also cottages alongside the former road that were summarily pulled down when the land was enclosed by the Leighs in the 1770s.

If Jane chose to take a shorter route home from New Road she would have turned up Main Street instead, probably more of a track until the major road alterations in 1803. Jane would not have witnessed the first thing that strikes a modern visitor— a small roofed shelter which houses one of the Great Western Railway's benches and the old British Rail station sign for Adlestrop. The station, which was located behind Tolsey Cottage was opened in 1853 and closed during Dr Beechings' massacre of the Victorian railway network in 1966 and all its buildings and platforms demolished leaving only the track. The village hall has a mural of the old station painted in 2000 to commemorate its existence. There are two stations still nearby, at Kingham and Moreton in Marsh on the Hereford and Worcester line that travels through Oxford up to Paddington. The Edward Thomas poem, 'Adlestrop' is engraved on a brass plaque on the bench upright and this has become a favourite place for tourists to take a photograph. Edward Thomas always carried a notebook with him for jotting down observations which might later be used for poetic inspiration. In his Field Note Books of 23-7 June 1914 (No. 75) he wrote:

24th
A glorious day from 4.20 a.m. & at 10 tiers above tiers of white cloud with dirtiest grey bars above the sea of slate

and dull brick by Battersea Pk – then at Oxford tiers of pure white with loose longer masses above and gaps of dark clear blue above haymaking and elms.

Then we stopped at Adlestrop, thro the willows cd be heard a chain of blackbird songs at 12.45 & one thrush & no man seen, only a hiss of engine letting off steam.

Stopping outside Campden by banks of long grass willow herb & meadowsweet, extraordinary silence between the two periods of travel – looking out on grey dry stones between metals & the shiny metals & over it all the elms willows & long grass – one man clears his throat — a greater than rustic silence.[6]

———

Let us return to our perambulation into the heart of Adlestrop up Main Street's gentle incline. At its end are two cottages covered with climbing roses in summertime beginning with The Old Post Office (now a bed & breakfast). You can still spot the old letter box with its 'GR' for King George V, alongside its front door. Next to it is Lob's Cottage and both are built in typical Cotswold style and their foundations could date back several hundred years. The row is now divided into two separate houses but once housed four families. The next detached house on this side of the road is Leigh Cottage, 17 Main Street, which, as proclaimed on its handsome scrolled crest on the front was built in 1868. Up to 1935 it was the first and original site for the village post office before this was moved to the bottom of the street, and boasted a public telephone and telegram service. Vine Cottage next door may be older than this – it is hard to know – and opposite it is Peartree Cottage, one of the oldest cottages remaining and typical of the labourer's cottages that Jane would have seen. Its roof was originally thatched and it also had a pretty thatched porch over the side doorway. It has tiny upstairs windows on the second floor in what were once attic bedrooms and its outer wall is held in place with a metal support. Inside the rooms are small and on different levels with thick stone walls, open hearths and stone flooring.

Its neighbour is a modern house built in the 1990s, Honeybrook Cottage, the name reflects the fact that the village brook winds behind the gardens before disappearing under the ground to come out at Marsh Bridge to join the Parish Brook. Adjacent to this are a pair of semi-detached stone houses (Numbers 4 and 3) which still have original Cotswold tiles on their roofs and handsome stone stoops over their front doors. Like Peartree Cottage their front doors are at the side of the house so it is probable that these houses were built before the upheavals of the 1800s. Opposite this on a high bank is number 15 Main Street, largely rebuilt in the last ten years which replaced an earlier thatched house. Many of the houses on this side of the street were built in the mid-nineteenth century – Laurel and Windrush House opposite the Post Office are dated 1843 and in common with many others have been enlarged and largely rebuilt in the last twenty years. They originally shared a porchway entrance with their front doors opening immediately into the front rooms. Most of the tenants of the nineteenth-century houses along here were farm workers and they had gardens planted with fruit trees – pears and apples – and stone outhouses where they could keep chickens or pigs. Whether this row replaced older cottages which helped house the villagers displaced by the enclosures and road buildings of the 1800s is impossible to say. A dusty track runs behind parallel to Main Street in between their back gardens and the old orchard.

One of the more intriguing buildings is the third and current Post Office site, a long thatched house that sits at the top of the sloping road. Its four cornered end is composed of red brick and stands out from the normal stonework. It may have been built as a cottage ornée with its wooden dripmoulds to the windows and wooden porch. Perhaps it was constructed as a scenic feature in the picturesque tradition in the eighteenth century by Sanderson Miller while working on Adlestrop House. In the 1870s it was home to three separate families – now it is divided into two with a room off the first cottage developed as a compact shop and post office. By the side is seating with chairs and tables offering tea and refreshments for walkers and visitors in the summer months. It flanks the small green, land not commonly owned but belonging to the Adlestrop Estate. A walnut tree has been planted in the centre, replacing an earlier one.

Apart from a small amount of traffic replacing the horses and carts and the tarmac sealing over the old white dusty limestone ways the peaceful village atmosphere still holds. The roads are too narrow and twisting to allow tourist coaches to intrude and there is nowhere for them to turn around. There are no yellow lines on the roads, no street lights and much of the old Adlestrop to enjoy. In February snowdrops cover the verges succeeded by daffodils before the May blossoming of cow parsley, comfrey, dandelions and daisies. It would not win a prize for 'best-kept' village, preferring to reflect its rural setting rather than present a more manicured appearance. Even the newer houses do not seem out of place since they are constructed with stone from the local quarries and ape the old building techniques.

What of the actual spirit of the village itself? Would Jane Austen find characters and a way of life at all similar to her own experiences? Despite its greatly diminished population since Jane Austen's day, there is certainly no shortage of interesting personalities in Adlestrop whose idiosyncracies nourish a little bit of gossipy conversation and offer food for thought. What can get overlooked in a large city is magnified in villages. Even among such a tiny community there are some lifelong simmering quarrels, stories of bitter arguments but also many more unsung acts of good neighbourliness. It really is a place where people are ready to help one another without even being asked – small and effective acts that seem to occur in a seamless way and village news, good or bad, is spread on a tide of conversation and now via email. Extreme weather such as the heavy snow of the winter of 2010-2011 or the floods of 2007 naturally foster this spirit of co-operation as do frequent water shortages and power cuts. Adlestrop can still appear to measure up to the dream of village life although this is a sentimental concept of the countryside that Jane Austen would never have indulged in.

It is a coincidence that this village has inspired two very different writers from different eras who both felt passionate about the English countryside. Edward Thomas, of course, only passed through Adlestrop Station but its atmosphere was enough to inspire him to use the name for his elegiac poem; Jane Austen knew the place far more intimately, although she never named it directly, and her family's deep roots within the village gave it extra resonance. As with the people she met, she was always careful to disguise her source material apart from obvious places like Bath or Lyme Regis which were essential to the plots. Adlestrop has almost become a metaphor for a country idyll and those who come here and write in the visitors' book kept in the church or pass through while walking, unaware they are treading in Jane Austen's footsteps, still find its quietness and its picturesque beauty a wholly satisfying experience.

Notes

Abbreviations

GA	Gloucester Archives
JASA	Jane Austen Society of Australia
Letter	These refer to the numbers given in *Jane Austen's Letters*, collected and edited by Deidre Le Faye, OUP, 1995
SBTRO	Shakespeare Birthplace Trust, Stratford on Avon

Chapter One

1 SBTRO 671/677
2 Letter 87, 15-16 September 1813 and Letter 98 5-8 March 1814
3 Letter 107, 9-18 September 1814
4 SBTRO 671/677
5 SBTRO DR 18/13/9/1
6 Darvill, *Prehistoric Gloucestershire*, (Chapter 4)
7 Grundy, *Saxon Charters and Field Names of Gloucestershire*
8 Austen-Leigh, *Jane Austen: Her Life and Letters – A Family Record* p6
9 Austen, 'My Aunt Jane Austen, A memoir' p9
10 SBTRO 671/677
11 Please see family trees to distinguish the different Leighs who bear the same Christian name
12 ibid.
13 Austen-Leigh, *Jane Austen: Her Life and Letters – A Family Record* p7
14 ibid.
15 SBTRO 671/677
16 SBTRO 671/677
17 Austen-Leigh, *Jane Austen Her Life and Letters: A Family Record* p9
18 SBTRO 671/677
19 *Persuasion*, Chapter 24

Notes

Chapter Two

1   SBTRO 671/677
2   ibid
3   SBTRO DR18/17/31/17a
4   Letter 64, 10-11 January 1809
5   Purcell, Mark, 'A lunatick of unsound mind': Edward, Lord Leigh (1742-86) and the refounding of Oriel College Library." *Bodleian Library Record*. Vol. 17, no. 3-4 (Apr-Oct 2001) p.247
6   ibid.
7   SBTRO, DR 671/33
8   Lane, *A Social History of Medicine* Chapter 6
9   Bearman (Ed.) *Stoneleigh Abbey, The House, Its Owners, Its Lands* Chapter 5
10 SBTRO DR 18/17/29/20
11 SBTRO DR 18/17/29/24
12 SBTRO DR 18/17/20/20-21
13 ibid.
14 Lane , *A Social History of Medicine* Chapter 6
15 SBTRO DR 18/17/27/171
16 *Mansfield Park*, Chapter 25
17 Collins, *Jane Austen and the Clergy*, p75
18 James Austen, *The Loiterer*, no.21
19 Letter 86 to Francis Austen 3-6 July 1813
20 SBTRO 671/677
21 ibid.
22 SBTRO DR 18/17/29/8
23 ibid.
24 *Frankenstein* by Mary Shelley, Chapter VI p.53
25 Letter from Lady Knatchbull to her sister, Marianne. First printed in the *Cornhill* magazine, 973,Winter 1947/8
26 Tomalin, *Jane Austen: A Life* p135
27 SBTRO 671/677
28 Austen, *My Aunt Jane Austen, A Memoir*, p11
29 Witts, *The Complete Diary of a Cotswold Lady*, February 10, 1789
30 Bearman (Ed.) *Stoneleigh Abbey: The House, Its Owners, Its Lands* Chapter 6, page 175
31 Letter 12, 1-2 December 1798
32 Letter 21, 11 June 1799
33 Letter 27, 20-21 November 1800
34 Letter 50, 8-9 February 1807
35 Letter 64, 10-11 January 1809
36 Letter 66, 24 January 1809
37 Letter 67, 30 January 1809

38 Letter 140, to Caroline Austen, 21 April 1816

Chapter Three

1   SBTRO, DR 671/677
2   ibid. NB Records state that this happened in 1768
3   ibid.
4   SBTRO 18/8/10/1
5   SBTRO 18/8/10/2-13
6   SBTRO DR 18/8/10/2
7   SBTRO 18/8/6/24
8   SBTRO 671/677
9   ibid.
10 ibid.
11 SBTRO, DR 18/17/29/15
12 ibid.
13 Batey, *Jane Austen and the English Landscape* p11
14 *The Daily Mail, 17.10.2009 Article by Ranulf Fiennes:* On 1 July 1788 the 13th Baron Saye & Sele killed himself in Harley Street, after failing to drown himself in gravel pits at Kensington, on being told there was no cure for his constant headaches by slashing his throat with a razor and falling on his regimental sword.
15 Le Faye, *Jane Austen's Letters, Bibliographical Index pp 581-2*
16 Letter 36, 12-13 May 1801
17 Witts, *The Complete Diary of a Cotswold Lady*, Volume 1, 9 January 1789
18 ibid, Volume 1, 21 January 1789
19 ibid, Volume 1, 12 August 1789
20 Leigh, *Bar, Bat & Bit*
21 Bearman (Ed.), *Stoneleigh Abbey: The House, Its Owners, Its Lands* Chapter 7

Chapter Four

1   Austen-Leigh, *A Memoir of Jane Austen and Other Family Recollections,* p26
2   *Northanger Abbey*, Chapter 20
3   Letter 6, 15-16 September 1796
4   Le Faye, *Jane Austen's 'Outlandish Cousin'* p144
5   ibid
6   Brill, *Life and Tradition in the Cotswolds*, p141
7   Beckinsale, *The English Heartland*, p 96
8   GA P5 M11
9   ibid.

10 SBTRO 18/8/16/8
11 ibid.
12 'Church History', John Gillett, 1992
13 *Mansfield Park*,Chapter 6
14 Lane, *Jane Austen's World*
15 'The Village Newsletter' December 2010/January 2011
16 *Mansfield Park*, Chapter 25
17 Jones, *A Thousand Years of the English Parish*, Chapter 10
18 SBTRO 671/77
19 ibid.
20 Note: Sir Edward Turner married Cassandra Leigh (James and Thomas' sister) and lived at Ambrosden in Oxfordshire. In the 1740s he replaced Ambrosden Manor House with a new building designed by Sanderson Miller. This was demolished by his son because it was thought too large.
21 SBTRO DR18/25/1
22 SBTRO DR 18/8/7/2
23 SBTRO DR 18/8/7
24 SBTRO 18/8/7/1
25 Verey, *The Buildings of England: Gloucestershire*
26 Warwickshire Records Office CR1382/1
27 'Church History', John Gillett, 1992
28 SBTRO 671/77
29 ibid.

Chapter Five

1   SBTRO 671/677
2   Letter 85, 24 May 1813
3   ibid.
4   *Emma*, Chapter 1
5   West, *Chaucer 1340-1400*, Chapter 8
6   Brill, *Life and Tradition on the Cotswolds*, p.110
7   Jones, *The Cotswolds*, Chapter 6
8   Brill, *Life and Tradition on the Cotswolds*, p.109
9   ibid Chapter 5
10 SBTRO DR 18/8/3/50
11 *Men and Armour for Gloucestershire in 1608* John Smith
12 Plumb, *England in the Eighteenth Century*
13 SBTRO DR 18/8/3/26
14 SBTRO DR 18/8/3/41
15 SBTRO 18/83/46
16 GA P5 M11

17 SBTRO DR18/8/7/3

18 SBTRO DR 18/8/3/45

19 Honan, *Jane Austen: Her Life*, Chapter 15 p260

20 Letter 77, 29-30 November 1812

21 SBTRO 18/8/10

22 Glos. Record Office D612 & Adlestrop Inclosure Act

23 SBTRO DR18/8/4/2

Chapter Six

1   Letter 104, 10-8 August 1814

2   Batey, *Jane Austen and the English Landscape*, p28ff

3   Batey, *The English Garden Tour: A View into the Past* p232

4   ibid (Bishop Porteus diary Vol 4, p3)

5   Duckworth, *The Improvements of the Estate*, Chapter 1

6   Wordsworth, *The Grasmere and Alfoxden Journals*, 15 April 1798 p152

7   VCH *A History of the County of Gloucester* Vol 6

8   GA D612/10

9   Beckinsale, *The English Heartland*, Chapter 10, p149

10 GA D610/T

11 GA DC 1100/1

12 SBTRO DR 18/8/7/12

13 Letter 39, 14 September 1804

14 'Taking the plunge: 18th century bath houses and plunge pools' Clare
    Hickman, *Historic Gardens* 2010

15 Repton, *Observations on the Theory and Practice of Landscape
    Gardening 1803* Chapter 3

16 *A Topographical and Historical Description of Gloucestershire*, 1815

Chapter Seven

1   SBTRO DR 671/36

2   SBTRO DR 18/29/6 (Box 1)

3   SBTRO DR 18/29/61

4   Purcell, Mark, "'A lunatick of unsound mind': Edward, Lord Leigh
    (1742-86) and the refounding of Oriel College Library" *Bodleian
    Library Record*. Vol. 17, no. 3-4 (Apr-Oct 2001) p. 246-260

5   SBTRO DR 671/77

6   Bearman (Ed.), *Stoneleigh Abbey: The House, Its owners, Its Lands.*
    Chapter 5

7   SBTRO DR 671/677 Letter dated 25 Feb 1792 from Hon. Mary Leigh to
    Joseph Hill

8   Spence, *A Century of Wills from Jane Austen's Family 1705-1806,* JASA

9   Bearman (Ed.) *Stoneleigh Abbey: The House,Its owners, Its Lands*, Chapter 5, p.155
10 ibid.
11 Letter 55, 30-June-1 July 1808
12 MS Pierpont Morgan Library, New York, holograph
13 SBTRO DR 18/17/32/41
14 Letter 55, 30-June-1 July 1808
15 Letter 61, 20 November 1808
16 Letter 86, 3-6 July 1813
17 SBTRO DR 18/17/39/5
18 ibid.
19 Duckworth, *The Improvement of the Estate* p87
20 Letter 157, 27 April 1817
21 'Jane Austen and the credit crunch of 1816' Markman Ellis, JA Society report 2011
22 Ibid.
23 Letter 157, 27 April 1817
24 Letter 86, 15-16 September 1813
25 Public Record Office

Chapter Eight

1   SBTRO DR 18/17/32/53
2   *Mansfield Park*, Chapter 8
3   ibid.
4   JA Papers
5   ibid.
6   Bearman (Ed.) *Stoneleigh Abbey: The House, its Owners, Its Lands,* Chapter 6, Page 176
7   *Mansfield Park,* Chapter 9
8   ibid.
9   *Diaries and Letters of Madame D'Arblay*, Charlotte Barrett (ed.) London 1842-6
10 Austen-Leigh, *Jane Austen – Her Life and Letters –A Family Record* p196-7
11 ibid.
12 Letter 43, 8-11 April 1805
13 ibid.
14 Bearman (Ed.) *Stoneleigh Abbey: The House, its Owners, Its Lands,* Chapter 6,
15 Letter 44, 21-23 April 1805

Notes

Chapter Nine

1   Maria Berry, *Extracts from the Journals and Correspondence of Miss Berry* ed. Lady Theresa Lewis, 3 vols, London (1865). Vol II, p434
2   Austen, *The Reminiscences of Caroline Austen*, Jane Austen Society 1986,21
3   SBTRO, DR 671/677
4   SBTRO 18/17/29-32
5   ibid.
6   SBTRO DR 671/769
7   *Mansfield Park*, Chapter 9
8   SBTRO, DR 671/769, p.19
9   Maria Berry, *Extracts from the Journals and Correspondence of Miss Berry from 1783-1852*, ed. Lady Theresa Lewis, 3 vols, London (1865). Vol II, p 433
10 ibid.
11 SBTRO DR 18/17/39/29
12 SBTRO DR 18/56/7 & DR 823/19
13 SBTRO DR 671/381
14 Bearman (Ed.), *Stoneleigh Abbey, The House, Its Owners, Its Lands* Chapter 4

Chapter Ten

1   Letter 79, 29 January 1813
2   *Mansfield Park*, Introduction by Tony Tanner (1966) p.31
3   Honan, *Jane Austen: Her Life*, Chapter 17
4   Collins, *Jane Austen and the Clergy*, p37
5   ibid, p37-39
6   James Austen, *Loiterer* No. 21
7   Austen-Leigh, *Jane Austen – Her Life and Letters – A Family Record* p9-10
8   Collins, *Jane Austen and The Clergy*, Chapter 2, pp 24-5
9   *The Life and Letters of William Cobbett in England and America*, pp 156-7
10 Letter 30, 8-9 January 1801
11 Atkyns, *The Ancient and Present State of Glostershire*, 1712
12 SBTRO DR 671/77
13 Letter 18, 21-23 January 1799
14 Collins, *Jane Austen and the Clergy*, Chapter 2, p44
15 Letter 32, 25 January 1801
16 Letter 33, 25 January 1801
17 SBTRO DR 18/17/32/97

Notes

18 Letter 67, 30 January 1809

19 Letter 58, 13 October 1808

20 Letter 59,15-16 October 1808

21 Letter 125 (A) 16 November 1815

22 Letter 132 (D)11 December 1815

Chapter Eleven

1   Witts, *The Complete Diary of a Cotswold Lady*, Volume 1, 12 May 1789

2   *Catharine* p187-8

3   Austen-Leigh, *Jane Austen – Her Life and letters – a Family Record* p10

4   Bence-Jones, *Clive of India*, page 220

5   Feiling, *Warren Hastings*, p40

6   Bernstein, *Dawning of the Raj: The Life and Trials of Warren Hastings*,Chapter 3

7   BL Add.MSS 29,174, f.25).

8   Eliza de Feuillide to Warren Hastings, 28 Dec 1797, R.A. Austen-Leigh *The Austen Papers, 1704-1856* p.32

9   Honan, *Jane Austen: Her Life*, Chapter Six, p.67-8

10 Letter 87 15-16 September 1813

11 SBTRO DR 671/677

12 ibid.

13 Lawson, *The Private Life of Warren Hastings, First Governor General of India*, 1895

14 Feiling, *Warren Hastings* p333

15 *The History of the Trial of Warren Hastings* Debrett, London, 1796

16 Witts, *The Complete Diary of a Cotswold Lady,* Vol 1 14 October 1789

17 *Mansfield Park*, Chapter 6

18 Mowl, *Historic Gardens of Gloucestershire* p105

19 Le Faye, *Jane Austen's 'Outlandish Cousin'* p145

20 Letter 55, 30 June-1 July 1808

21 This painting is now in the Paul Mellon Collection at the Yale Center for British Art in Connecticut.

22 Feiling, *Warren Hastings*, Chapter 28

Chapter Twelve

1   'Church History', John Gillett, 1992

2   Cholmondeley, *Adlestrop, Its Cottages and their Inmates*, p7

3   VCH, British History, Parishes: Adlestrop

4   Cholmondeley, *Adlestrop, Its Cottages and their Inmates,* p12

5   Hartman, *The Remainder Biscuit,* p66

6   Harvey, *Adlestrop Revisited*, p11

Bibliography

Austen, Caroline 'My Aunt Jane Austen, a memoir'. Winchester, Jane Austen Society, 2008

Austen-Leigh, William and Richard, *Jane Austen – Her Life and Letters – A Family Record*. New York, E.P. Dutton & Company, 1913

Batey, Mavis, *Jane Austen and the English Landscape*. London, Barn Elms Publishing, 1996

Batey, Mavis and Lambert, David, *The English Garden Tour: A View into the Past*. London, John Murray, 1990

Bearman, Robert (Ed.) *Stoneleigh Abbey: The House, Its Owners, Its Lands*. Warwickshire, Stoneleigh Abbey Ltd in association with The Shakespeare Birthplace Trust, 2004

Beckinsale, Robert & Monica, *The English Heartland*. London, Duckworth, 1980

Bence-Jones, Mark, *Clive of India*. London, Constable, 1974

Bernstein, Jeremy, *Dawning of the Raj: The Life & Trials of Warren Hastings*. London, Aurum Press, 2001

Brill, Edith, *Life and Tradition on the Cotswolds*. Gloucestershire, Amberley, 2009

Brayley, E.W. & Britton, J, *A Topographical and Historical Description of the County of Gloucester*. 1815

Cholmondeley, Rose Evelyn,*Adlestrop, Its Cottages and their Inmates 1876-77*. Oxford, The Shakespeare Head Press, 1935

Collins, Irene, *Jane Austen and the Clergy*. London, The Hambledon Press, 1993

The Country Houses of Gloucestershire Vols 1-3. Chichester, Phillimore 1989-2001

Darvill, Timothy, *Prehistoric Gloucestershire: Forests and Vales and High Blue Hills*. (2nd edition). Stroud, Amberley, 2011

Defoe, Daniel, *A Tour Through the Whole Island of Great Britain*. London, Penguin Classic, 1986

Duckworth, Alistair M, *The Improvement of the Estate: A Study of Jane Austen's Novels*. Baltimore & London, John Hopkins University Press, 1994

Edwards, Anne-Marie, *In the Steps of Jane Austen: Walking Tours of Austen's England*. Wisconsin, Jones Books, 2003

Fraser, Flora, *The Unruly Queen: The Life of Queen Caroline*. London,Macmillan, 1996

Grundy, G.B., *Saxon Charters and Field Names of Gloucestershire*. Bristol and

Bibliography

Gloucestershire Archaeological Society, 1935

Harvey, Anne, *Adlestrop Revisited*. Stroud, Sutton Publishing, 1999

Hartman, Robert, *The Remainder Biscuit*. London, André Deutsch, 1964

Honan, Park, *Jane Austen: Her Life*. London, Weidenfeld & Nicolson,1987

'Inclosure in Gloucestershire'. Gloucester Records Office, 1976

Jenkins, Elizabeth, *Jane Austen, A Biography*. London, Sphere,1972

Jones, Anthea, *The Cotswolds*. Chichester, Phillimore, 1994

Jones, Anthea, *A Thousand Years of the English Parish*. Moreton-in-Marsh, The Windrush Press, 2000

Lane, Joan, *A Social History of Medicine: Health, Healing and Disease in England*. London, Routledge, 2001

Lane, Maggie, *Jane Austen's World: The Life and Times of England's Most Popular Novelist*. London, Carlton Books, 1996

Le Faye, Deidre, *Jane Austen's 'Outlandish Cousin'*. London, The British Library, 2002

Le Faye, Deidre, *Jane Austen: Writer's Lives*. London, The British Library, 1998

Le Faye, Deidre, *Jane Austen's Letters*. (Collected and edited) Oxford, OUP, 1995

Leigh, Sir Edward Chandos, *Bar, Bat & Bit*. London,1913

Men and Armour for Gloucestershire in 1608. Gloucester, Alan Sutton, 1980

Mingay, G.E.,*English Landed Society in the Eighteenth Century*. London, Routledge, Kegan, Paul,1963

Mowl, Timothy, *Historic Gardens of Gloucestershire*. Stroud, Tempus, 2002

Ortigo, Iris, *The Merchant of Prato: Daily Life in a Medieval Italian City*. London, Penguin, 1992

Pevsner, Nikolaus (Ed.) & Verey, David, *Gloucestershire:The Cotswolds, The Buildings of England*.Middlesex, Penguin Books, 1970

Pevsner, Nikolaus (Ed.) & Wedgwood, Alexandra, *Warwickshire, The Buildings of England*. Middlesex, Penguin Books, 1966

Plumb, J.H., *England in the Eighteenth Century*. Middlesex, Penguin Books, 1950

Tomalin, Claire, *Jane Austen, A Life*. London, Viking, 1997

Spence, Jon, *A Century of Wills from Jane Austen's Family*. Jane Austen Society of Australia

Spence, Jon, *The Leighs: The Revelations of Stoneleigh*. Jane Austen Society of Australia

Watson, J. Steven, *The Reign of George III 1760-1815*. Oxford, OUP, 1960

West, Richard, *Chaucer: The Life and Times of the First English Poet*. London, Constable, 2000

Witts, Agnes, *The Complete Diary of a Cotswold Lady: The Lady of Rodborough. Volume 1 1788-1793*. Ed. Alan Sutton, Gloucestershire, Amberley, 2011

Wordsworth, Dorothy, *The Grasmere and Alfoxden Journals*. Oxford, OUP, 2002

Index

Index

Step back into a time of Georgian elegance and walk in the footsteps of

Jane Austen

at

Stoneleigh Abbey

Check our website for details
www.stoneleighabbey.org